Women in Educational
Management

OPEN UNIVERSITY PRESS
Gender and Education Series
Editors
ROSEMARY DEEM
Professor of Educational Research, University of Lancaster
GABY WEINER
Principal Lecturer in Education at South Bank University

The series provides compact and clear accounts of relevant research and practice in the field of gender and education. It is aimed at trainee and practising teachers, and parents and others with an educational interest in ending gender inequality. All age-ranges will be included, and there will be an emphasis on ethnicity as well as gender. Series authors are all established educational practitioners or researchers.

TITLES IN THE SERIES

Boys Don't Cry
Sue Askew and Carol Ross

Science and Technology in the Early Years
Naima Browne (ed.)

Untying the Apron Strings
Naima Browne and Pauline France (eds)

Changing Perspectives on Gender
Helen Burchell and Val Millman (eds)

Co-education Reconsidered
Rosemary Deem (ed.)

Women Teachers
Hilary de Lyon and Frances Widdowson Migniuolo (eds)

Girls and Sexuality
Lesley Holly (ed.)

Women in Educational Management
Jenny Ozga (ed.)

A History of Women's Education in England
June Purvis

Shaping Up to Womanhood
Sheila Scraton

Whatever Happens to Little Women?
Christine Skelton (ed.)

Dolls and Dungarees
Eva Tutchell (ed.)

Just a Bunch of Girls
Gaby Weiner (ed.)

Women and Training
Ann Wickham

Women in Educational Management

Edited by Jenny Ozga

Open University Press
Buckingham • *Philadelphia*

Open University Press
Celtic Court
22 Ballmoor
Buckingham
MK18 1XW

and
1900 Frost Road, Suite 101
Bristol, PA 19007, USA

First Published 1993

A catalogue record of this book is available
from the British Library

Library of Congress Cataloging-in-Publication Data

Women in educational management / edited by Jenny Ozga.
     p.   cm. — (Gender in education series)
    Includes index.
    ISBN 0–335–09340–X (pbk)
    1. Women school administrators—Great Britain. 2. School
management and organization—Great Britain. I. Ozga, Jenny.
II. Series
LB2831.826.G72W66 1992
371.2'0082—dc20   92–17389
                                         CIP

Typeset by Colset Private Limited, Singapore
Printed in Great Britain by J.W. Arrowsmith Limited, Bristol

Contents

Series Editor's Introduction

Jenny Ozga's book is a timely and very welcome addition to our series. In the last few years there has been much discussion about the need for 'more and better' management in schools, colleges and higher education. In many countries this has been connected with a perceived contemporary crisis in educational establishments and it has also often been underscored by a market ideology which likens schools to businesses. With a few exceptions however, the management lobby has largely ignored the issues of gender and race and the power relations underlying these divisions and hence has neglected to explore the difficulties, including absence of appropriate childcare, sex discrimination and sexual harassment, facing managers who are female and/or black. At the same time there has been little analysis of the different perspectives and values which women managers may bring to their task.

This collection will fulfil two significant purposes. First it offers valid and important documentation of the experiences of women managers in education, demonstrating their strengths and achievements as well as their struggles. Second, it provides support and illumination for other women in education who take on management roles, showing that it is possible for women to develop management strategies which do not ape the aggressive, competitive, hierarchical approach favoured by many male managers.

The biographies of the women who have contributed to this collection vary greatly, but all of them show courage, dedication, energy and considerable commitment to the furtherance of student learning and equal opportunities through schooling.

Furthermore, they demonstrate conclusively the truth and strength of the feminist phrase 'the personal is the political'.

The book, although drawing in one or two cases on small scale research, does not set out to offer research evidence and findings but the writings and experiences included here will provide rich food for the thoughts of those who wish to develop such research. The gender structuring of organizations which the chapters document ought also to make all of us reconsider the places in which we work, their characteristic mode of operation and the future agendas for change which we draw up.

If the inspiration provided by the collection enables women who work in education to establish, foster and develop educational institutions in which values of social justice are uppermost, then this will surely prove to have been a very valuable step forward in the creation of a less sexist and racist world.

Rosemary Deem

Introduction: In a Different Mode

JENNY OZGA

Aims of the book

This book is mainly about women who are managers in the education service, though it also takes a brief look at ways of encouraging women to become managers – through training courses, for example. But most of it is taken up with accounts by women of how they developed their 'careers': the routes – often circuitous – which they followed to get where they are now, the combinations of accident and design which led to their current management positions. These are accounts of lives as well as careers, for women often do not have access to the experience of unilinear career progression open to men, nor do they choose to pursue such limited versions of career development. The accounts are, of course, intended 'to encourage others', but they are not the stories of superwomen; they show that women can find satisfactory career paths, that they can balance the various demands made on them, even in a society which, at best, provides no practical assistance and at worst actively discriminates against them. Some of the accounts illustrate the barriers to progression, and these cover incidences of discrimination – for example, the refusal of superiors or appointing committees to recognize ability in a woman – but they also deal with the problems of meeting domestic 'obligations', which, for women, often include the obligation to renounce a career in favour of one's partner's and to take primary (i.e. all) responsibility for childcare. Other accounts demonstrate the strength and imagination of women who find ways of self-development within the constraints imposed by prejudice and domestic 'choice'. All the accounts demonstrate the qualities which women develop in their working and other lives.

As well as providing accounts which other women will recognize, the contributors talk about the ways in which they define and carry out their management functions. For not only are women managers largely absent from a service in which they form the majority of the workforce, management as practised by women is also absent from discussions of educational management, whether that is located in training courses, in local or central-government policy documents, or in academic research and publications. Education management, like management elsewhere, is largely done by men, and is therefore defined by men. Such a definition may be very restricted: at best it may be inappropriate for women; at worst it is hostile to the fostering of management qualities which may represent more ethical and also more effective ways of managing people – and managing people is what educational management is primarily about.

The two strands of the book – the accounts of women's complex 'careers' and of their particular management styles and practices – run together and reinforce one another. It is the complex, varied and rich experience of women's lives which develops their particular management styles and capacities. Men, who are excluded from such experience or who perceive it as low-status and valueless, do not develop such skills, and therefore exclude them from conventional management practice, from the very definition of what constitutes management. However, we have to be cautious here. The accounts stress barriers, roundabout routes, horizontal 'career' routes, choices, pressures, problems. They also, as I have said, reveal strengths, and the development of ways of doing things which are more likely to be characteristic of women than of men. From there is but a short step to the argument that adversity is character-forming, challenges are good for you, and the rich variety of women's lives (i.e. the double-shift of work and housework/care) had better be maintained if we are to continue to develop such rich, multi-dimensional management styles. That of course, is not the message that this collection intends to put across. The emphasis here is on the positive: the possibility of 'success' being defined in ways which do not oblige a woman to be more like a man but which permit the development of management styles that are appropriate for, and acceptable to, people. We have an enormous opportunity in educational management at the moment, in that, for unprincipled, pragmatic reasons, shortage of skilled labour should help greatly in the removal of barriers to women's advancement in management, where years of principled appeals to justice and fairness have failed. Much more needs to be done to make this possible, and the accounts collected here review some of the areas which need urgent attention. But the opportunity will have been missed if women's increased presence in educational management makes no difference to management practice, if women are simply absorbed into management and become indistinguishable from men. This book, then, is proposing two connected sets of arguments, summarized below:

1 Women are absent from educational management: they are the exception when they might be expected to be the rule. Their absence is caused by structural, societal obstacles to their advancement, yet some women display a great determination and imagination and develop satisfactory 'careers'. Much more needs to be done to break down obstacles to women's advancement, and to combat discrimination against women. At the same time, the concept of 'career' itself needs redefinition so as to include women's experience, with the intention of retaining the richness and diversity of women's definitions of 'career' without the embittering, frustrating and exhausting experience that results from constantly hitting obstacles or encountering discrimination.
2 Just as 'career' needs redefining, so too does 'good management practice'. Much management is preoccupied with practices more likely to be experienced and valued by men. Women's experiences incline them towaids management practice which is not recognized as appropriate by men, and when women become managers they often have to take on definitions of management which exclude their experience and their understanding, or they face yet another struggle to have their ways of working accepted.

Redefinition of both 'career' and 'management' would not only benefit women – though that would be no small thing – it would benefit people: those in educational management and those managed.

In the remainder of the Introduction, I want to look in more detail at some of the issues I have just raised, under the following headings:

- the absence of women from educational management and explanations of it;
- the nature of a 'female management style' and how it may differ from conventional management.

The absence of women from educational management

The extent of the absence

Women form the majority of the workforce in education; they are underrepresented in its management. This is the case in all sectors, and in all developed countries. Women are more visible in the management of education offered to younger pupils: as the age of pupils increases, the proportion of women diminishes. In higher education – especially in the universities – women managers are such a small proportion of management that they are almost invisible. The same holds true in the arenas of local- and central-government management and policy-making in education: there has been a handful of women Ministers, and a growing minority of women Senior Education Officers and civil servants in many western countries; however it could be argued that women have gained access to such posts just as the importance of the posts has diminished.

Information on the distribution of promoted posts by gender is rather out of date (Figures 1 and 2; Tables 1 and 2), as we do not have figures which cover the restructured teaching profession of England and Wales. There are some (informal) indications that the distribution of allowances may have exacerbated the disadvantaged position of women in teaching.

Explanations of women's absence from management

There is a range of explanations of women's absence from management, reflecting different perspectives on the issue. These range from deficit theories – i.e. those that stress women's inadequacy or incapacity – to more structural explanations which stress issues of power and control and the patriarchal construction of society. Assumptions about women's inadequacies permeated literature on teaching and education management, perhaps especially in the 1950s and 1960s, but there is very little research evidence to support them – although explanations couched in such terms may still be found in some surprising places. They rest on 'common-sense' explanations and notions of

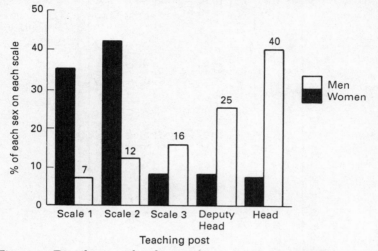

Figure 1   Distribution of scale posts by sex in primary schools (DES 1985, Table B129).

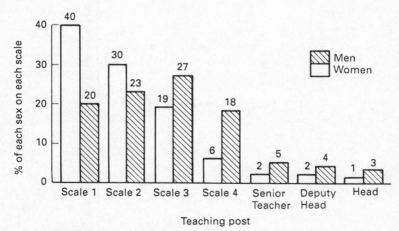

Figure 2   Distribution of scale posts by sex in secondary schools (DES 1985, Table B129).

Table 1   Percentages of men and women teachers on different pay scales, 1981 and 1987

	Primary				Secondary			
	Men		Women		Men		Women	
	1981	1987	1981	1987	1981	1987	1981	1987
Head	30.16	32.20	6.98	7.35	3.19	3.43	0.74	0.79
Deputy Head	17.83	19.94	8.17	8.13	4.05	4.71	2.20	2.35
Second Master and Senior Teacher	0.47	0.33	0.25	0.14	4.24	5.57	2.75	2.47
Scale 4	0.22	0.39	0.06	0.11	6.63	18.81	5.69	6.76
Scale 3	11.60	12.07	7.09	7.23	25.07	28.16	17.79	21.04
Scale 2	28.85	25.17	41.64	39.18	24.65	22.50	28.63	30.18
Scale 1	10.87	9.90	35.82	37.85	20.82	16.80	42.20	36.36
Total no.	43,323	35,947	145,144	138,329	134,009	120,843	110,494	106,771

Source: DES (1989) Statistics of Education.

Table 2   Percentages of men and women secondary teachers on different pay scales, March 1988

	Men		Women	
	Full-time	Part-time	Full-time	Part-time
Head	4	1	1	–
Deputy Head	7	–	4	–
Main scale with:				
Incentive allowance:				
E	6	2	2	–
D	21	7	8	–
C	2	1	2	–
B	26	10	22	1
A	3	4	4	1
No incentive allowance	31	63	57	91
Other scales	–	13	1	7
Total	100	100	100	100
All teachers (thousands)	103.0	3.6	88.4	26.0

Source: DES *Survey of Secondary Staffing.*

what is appropriate and 'feminine'. On the other hand, there has
been research aimed at identifying the barriers and structural
conditions which impede women's advancement (see, for example Sikes *et al.* 1985), and a good deal has been done to reveal the
extent of their effects. Research which draws on women's experiences and their own explanations of career 'choice' is beginning to
appear and makes a significant contribution, as it recasts some of
the deficit explanations in ways which reveal the impact of barriers. For example, it does seem to be the case that women put
themselves forward for promotion less often than men; this
results from a combination of women's realistic grasp of what is
possible in a discriminatory system, a tendency to be scrupulous
about self-evaluation and an antipathy to the way school management is presented and constructed. Structural explanations
which emphasize male hegemony allow for the reinterpretation
of much of the existing material about women's absence in such a
way as to avoid 'blaming the victim'.

There is an enormous literature on gender inequality, its
causes, its effects and ways of combating it. I cannot possibly
review it all here, but I would like to point to the connections

between that general literature, and the stages in its development, and the literature on women and educational management.

Very briefly, literature on gender inequality reflects the variety of perspectives mentioned above; that is, it ranges from literature which depends on some notion of 'given' or biologically determined male and female characteristics and roles exercised in appropriate masculine (public) and feminine (private) spheres, to literature which emphasizes the processes of socialization into such roles. The concept of patriarchy has been used to draw attention to the fact that the preservation of a public/private division, and of male and female characteristics/roles, is necessary for the preservation of male hegemony, and is both a consequence and a cause of that hegemony. The first type of approach explains women's absence from positions of power in terms of their inadequacy and incapacity; the second stresses the barriers to their advancement – barriers which include the inculcation of 'feminine' qualities by the socialization process, and the exclusion of these qualities from masculine, public-sphere activities. These barriers also include the interest of most men in the preservation of a status quo which favours them, and women's perceptions of their unequal status and of masculine definitions of management as 'natural'.

There are two further, and positive, developments which need to be mentioned here. The first concerns research on organizational structures which helps to move us forward beyond the recognition of patriarchy's pervasiveness and the helplessness or despair that such recognition may bring. Focusing on the structures themselves as 'problems', in terms of the ways they buttress male power, opens up the possibility of restructuring so as to accommodate or encourage women. Rosabeth Moss Kanter's *Men and Women of the Corporation* (1977: 246) demonstrated how organizational structures and divisions in the USA discriminate against women and black people: 'Opportunity, power and relative numbers . . . have the potential to explain a large number of discrete individual responses to organisations.' Work done since then (in North America) documents the increase in applications for management positions from women when organizational barriers are removed. The appointment of women to senior posts acts as a powerful stimulus for more women to apply (Edson 1981; Pitner 1981).

The second positive aspect of current developments in research on gender issues concerns the recognition of the complexities surrounding socialization and the construction of public and private spheres. The evidence of women's deliberate and informed rejection of male roles and masculine behaviours raises complex questions. It is not sufficient to reject the notion of inherent 'feminine' qualities, especially those of compliance and submission, as this could lead to an undervaluing of qualities encouraged by female socialization and a overvaluing of masculine, public-sphere behaviour. This in turn could lead to an emphasis on strategies for change which encourage women to adopt masculine behaviours and values – to be competitive, aggressive; to look like men – as evidenced in their crassest form in the wave of 1980s advertising, films and pulp fiction featuring power-dressed women executives.

The recognition that women make an informed choice not to enter management because 'the price is too high' has implications for strategies for women's advancement in management: it moves us on from the need to remove structural barriers (though that need remains) to the need to redefine what counts as good management practice. In the next section I want to look at how management in education has been defined, at the ways in which it excludes women's experiences, and at possibilities for identifying and fostering women's management styles and practices.

Conventional approaches to educational management

As with the literature on gender inequality, there is not the space here to review the educational management literature. It is sizeable, though its quality is questionable – not just in relation to its androcentricity but in its long history of uncritical acceptance of inappropriate approaches from other areas of work. Its production has become something of an industry in itself, especially in North America, though in England the 1988 Education Reform Act (ERA) has also boosted the production and sales of management manuals for a new breed of autonomous school-based Chief Executive.

I have written elsewhere (Ozga and Westoby 1989) about the inadequacies of much of this literature and the approaches that it represents. At its best it is little more than common sense, and education managers who are operating without some of the systematic management processes that they find presented in the major texts probably shouldn't be in their posts. At its worst it presents Heads with blueprints for leadership which fail to recognize the policy context of the school and which are in general abstracted from the educational setting and function. They require Heads to produce 'clear aims and goals', refusing to recognize that these are not immediately and blindingly obvious in education, where, for example, the clear aim of academic success may conflict with the clear aim of good vocational and technical provision.

The conventional literature's tendency to disengage itself from the really hard questions facing educational managers, while at the same time emphasizing 'leadership' as the key factor in the successful educational enterprise, has placed a heavy burden on those Heads who accept the message in the texts, but it has left something of a void for those who are dissatisfied with it but are looking for guidance and assistance with managing education (rather than budgets, or plant, or perfect machine bureaucracies, or marketing agencies). Some of the criticisms made of conventional literature connect to feminist critiques of that literature, while feminist work on women managers suggests that there are alternatives to current theory and practice which could support thoughtful women *and* men.

The androcentric bias of educational management is but a single instance of the creation of knowledge and culture in exclusive terms; as Smith has (famously) put it (1987: 283):

> What is there – spoken sung, written, made emblematic in art – and treated as general, universal, unrelated to a particular position or a particular sex as its source and standpoint, is in fact partial, limited, located in a particular position and permeated by special interests and concerns.

A brief consideration of the literature on leadership and motivation (which has a continued powerful presence in recent texts, even though much of the original research is ageing) illustrates the extent to which its concepts are stereotypically masculine. Leadership is typically authoritarian, charismatic or entrepreneurial; motivation is typically competitive, and linked to success defined as winning, as beating down the opposition – explained by the superiority of 'self-actualising' rather than 'affiliative' needs in Maslow's hierarchy. (See Shakeshaft 1989: 148–66 for a fuller discussion of this theme.)

The beginnings of research on women's management and leadership styles suggest that there are differences from this conventional model (Neville 1988). Women's leadership style is less hierarchical and more democratic. Women, for example, run more closely knit schools than do men, and communicate better with teachers. They use different, less dominating, body language and different language and procedures. Women appear more flexible and sensitive, and often more successful. Pitner's (1981) detailed study of the leadership styles of male and female School Superintendents in North America showed that women spent less time on deskwork than men, visited more classrooms, kept up to date on curricular issues, spent more time with their peers and sponsored other women. Their language was more hesitant and tentative, their agendas more informal and flexible, and there was less distance from subordinates.

Other recognizable differences include the following:

- *Definitions of task* Women emphasize cohesiveness. They are much less individualistic, and spend time on fostering an integrative culture and climate.
- *Stress/conflict management* Women cope more readily with 'routine' stress, and defuse conflict. They do not engage in displays of anger as control mechanisms (and hence may be mistakenly judged as 'weak').
- *Group management* Group activities are much more highly valued by women than by men. Men attempt to retain control in group situations, or they withdraw.

These characteristics fit well with recent descriptions of progressive industrial management; they fit with organic rather than mechanistic views of organization. Indeed, there is much to suggest that such flexible, supportive and integrative approaches are of particular value in education (though that does not exclude a more general applicability).

Meanwhile the educational policy context looks unpromising for the woman manager or would-be manager committed to constructing good practice in an unconventional, 'female' mode. Post-ERA management structures privilege efficiency and entrepreneurialism, while reduced resources, increased competition between providers, and tighter prescription of the content of schooling reduce the scope for humane and integrative educational leadership. For it is not simply that 'male' and 'female' management *styles* differ: those styles are predicated on different values.

There may be some indicators, however, that a fruitful relationship between female management and progressive industrial practice could develop in education and other public services. Wider participation in education may bring more flexible provision and with it more respect for different students' differing needs and experiences and less respect for the old (male) disciplines. In a period where certainties and structures are disappearing, the need for solidarity is all the greater. Where the really difficult problems in education are increasingly acute, the more apparent is the need for management to be value-driven, to nurture and support staff and enhance their self-worth, and to operate ethically. How else can difficult choices be made, and difficult problems be tackled, without damage to the people who work in education, as well as to those who manage them? The 1980s saw a considerable amount of that damage in many western countries. More than ever, educational managers need a vocabulary through which they can communicate about educational issues, and a management style which encompasses democratic and educative principles. Some of that language and style is more readily available to women: they retain and promote its use even in a climate where equality of opportunity is redefined as 'choice' or 'parity of esteem' revisited.

Conclusion – a personal note

Some of the contributors to this collection have pointed out to me that it was unfair that they should be asked to consider their careers, to revisit painful episodes in their lives and to discuss their management principles in a public arena, while I collected that material and said nothing about my own practice. I take the point. In thinking about this section of the introductory chapter I have come to appreciate the difficulty of the task with which I presented my contributors. I had no right to expect them to reveal their difficulties without revealing my own, nor to ask them to attempt to define their management styles without attempting the task myself. If they were sufficiently courageous not to be intimidated by the likely response from colleagues, then I should be too, despite misgivings about hostages to fortune.

I am now a manager, though I never embarked on a career in management. My relationship with educational management has always been, and remains, ambivalent, as I have considerable experience of researching it, teaching and writing about it, but only intermittent experience of practising it – at least until recently.I am committed to management which is firmly rooted in principled academic practice, to management which is designed to achieve agreed and negotiated educational aims. Such management requires effective and enabling organizational structures, but it also requires an enabling and secure culture and climate. The difficulty of establishing such a climate and culture should not be underestimated. There are many obstacles, including the distrust and anxiety produced by the external context. Such a context can produce pressures for the kind of stereotypical 'leadership' which is criticized earlier in this Introduction. It is often difficult to resist such pressures, particularly when the effort to encourage others to take ownership of policy development seems so great, and that ownership itself is so fragile in the face of the threats of externally imposed change. I have also had to struggle with my impatience, and with my tendency to assume that my aims are widely shared and widely understood. It has been particularly difficult for me to accept that in my determined pursuit of shared ownership of the Faculty's policy-making processes I have employed strategies as apparently autocratic and intolerant as any conventional (male) manager.

However, despite the difficulties, I remain convinced of the virtues of 'female' management styles, recognizing that I aspire to the best of them, rather than that I have any 'natural' claims to them. I have a great deal of stereotypical behaviour to unlearn, no less than my male colleagues. However, changes are being made, with the support of colleagues who are receptive to my intentions if critical of some of the execution. The women with whom I work seem to have greater ease in critically reviewing our performance – perhaps, as women, we are more inclined to be self-critical – but we are evolving as a supportive and sustaining group. However challenging the attempt, and however frustrating, it seems to us that there is no viable alternative. Given the uncertainty of the context and the anxiety of colleagues, the need to build consensus and gain access to expertise and initiative at all levels in the organization is self-evident.

The Open University was the organization which had the most

profound effect on my thinking about management. Because it is an institution which, at its best, operates both creatively and efficiently, it contains – in its idealized modes, at least – the essence of good educational management process. The design of courses is a team-based activity, in which authority is not hier-archical but relates to the capacity to argue a case. The produc-tion process imposes a framework for the activity of disparate and creative professionals, and imposes a discipline which causes stress but also produces effective material. At its best, the organi-zation of a group of creative and committed people with the aim of producing excellent teaching materials suggests possibilities for all creative/educational organizations, or at least suggests certain guiding principles. I recognize that the picture is idealized, but at the same time it is undoubtedly the case that the balance of con-trol and autonomy, so essential in the creative functioning of organizations, is nearer achievement in the OU than in many other educational organizations.

From the OU I learned the importance of clearly stated and widely shared educational aims and objectives, without which the most efficient educational organization has neither meaning nor force. I also learned that work done in groups where think-ing was shared was often painful and slow, but more durable and of better quality than work done more rapidly by talented individuals who were unprepared to accept the discipline of the group. Teaching educational management through such means was often an illuminating process, though not always by design.

I learned a number of harder lessons in my career at the OU and elsewhere. Among them were lessons about the limits of tolerance of principles expressed forcefully by a woman, and about expectations and assumptions about the career/promotion prospects of a woman with young children. These hard lessons were dispiriting, but they also made me angry on my own account and on behalf of others, and I came to appreciate and learn from the support and example of other women. Without that support I would probably still have tried to convince myself that the 'fault' lay somewhere in me, and not in the prejudice which I encoun-tered. As a rational person, readily committed to processes of evaluation and measurement of performance, it took me a long time to admit that there was no explanation on performance grounds for my 'failure' and the advancement of others, and as a woman, albeit a forceful one, it took me even longer to become constructively angry about it. The anger remains, and fuels my determination to develop and sustain a management ethos which builds on existing good practice and commitment to equality of opportunity. I am fortunate in the support I receive towards the achievement of those aims from my own management and from my colleagues.

All the contributors to this book share the broad aims of enhancement of opportunity for women in educational management. That shared commitment stems from experience of overcoming barriers; from experience of conventional, inefficient management; from taken-for-granted assumptions about sensible and humane ways of getting things done. We do not suggest that women have a 'natural' capacity to manage better, but we do submit that the styles of communication and organization with which women are familiar are effective management styles, with particular application in education.

References

DES (1985) *Statistics on Teachers In Service*. London, HMSO.

DES (1989) *Statistics of Education*. London, HMSO.

Edson, S.K. (1981) 'If they can, I can: women aspirants to administrative positions in public schools' in P. Schmuck *et al.* (eds) *Education Policy and Management: Sex Differentials*. New York, Academic Press.

Kanter, R.M. (1977) *Men and Women of the Corporation*. New York, Basic Books.

Neville, M. (1988) *Promoting Women: Successful Women in Educational Management*. Auckland, Longman Paul.

Ozga, J. and Westoby, A. (1989) *Education Organizations and Professionals*, E814 Study Guide. Milton Keynes, OUEE.

Pitner, N. (1981) 'Hormones and harems: are the activities of superintending different for a woman?' in P. Schmuck *et al.* (eds) *Education Policy and Management: Sex Differentials*. New York, Academic Press.

Shakeshaft, C. (1989) *Women in Educational Administration*. London, Sage.

Sikes, P., Measor, L. and Woods, P. (1985) *Teachers' Lives: Crises and Continuities*. Lewes, Falmer.

Smith, S. (1987) 'A peculiar eclipsing: women's exclusion from man's culture' *Women's Studies Institutional Quarterly*, 1(4), 281–96.

CHAPTER 1

Black Women in Educational Management

CAS WALKER

Women in management and managerial positions are subject to pressures and experiences which are not experienced by men; on the other hand, it can be argued that they share some of the same work-related pressures as their male counterparts. In a similar way black women in management, while sharing some of the same experiences as other women managers, are subject to other experiences which are unique to themselves.

Despite the many changes which have taken place in education in recent years, women in management positions are still in a minority. Black women in these positions therefore find themselves as a small group within that female minority. Because women in these positions are so few, certain specific pressures can be identified as having an effect on their performance. These pressures include feelings of isolation, the strain of coping with sex stereotyping, discrimination from colleagues, and the whole experience of pressure from an institutional culture. All these can lead to great levels of stress.

This chapter will explore the specific pressures in relation to the experiences of black women. It will highlight some of the situations which cause stress and go on to describe some of the ways in which these have been handled. A small number of black women were interviewed to identify pressures in relation to their own background and career. The women were interviewed either in their school or at home. Informal discussions were also held with another group. All of these women live and work in the West Midlands. The interviews were informal, with mainly open-ended questions being asked covering career development and progression as well as their current management experience.

The respondents speak for themselves throughout this chapter.

Black women in educational management now exist at a variety of levels – as Faculty Heads, Heads of Department, Headteachers at primary and secondary levels, Assistant Principals, Heads of Units, and Heads of Support Services, and also as LEA advisers/inspectors, Assistant Education Officers, members of HM Inspectorate and a recently appointed Chief Education Officer. It must be said that these women are few in comparison to other women in similar educational management positions, and this reflects the position of black women managers in other professions.

On the positive side, the importance of having role models is well-documented, and the mere existence of these women holds out hope for other black women. However, if we look at isolation as a factor which can cause stress, most of the black women in any of these positions are entirely isolated either in terms of race or by gender. Difficulties related to isolation or exclusion are widespread, but the women in this study wanted to share them so that they could be recognized by others, and also be recognized as not insurmountable. Some of the major problems and barriers stemmed from the nature of early immigration to Britain, and the ways in which black women were channelled into particular jobs – especially as 'carers' and 'servers'. Even educated women faced exclusion from the teaching labour-market in Britain. Here is someone reflecting on her early encounter with the education system:

> The first barrier was getting the job in the education system in England. Though I was a qualified teacher, I could not get into education for over two years after I came from India.
>
> (A Headteacher)

Although the immigrant communities placed a great value on education as one of the ways in which their members would be able to gain some degree of status in British society, there were many barriers to their acceptance, let alone advancement. This happened despite the fact that some of these women had teaching qualifications or other experience of working in education. These women were the product of a colonial education system mainly based on the British model. Post-colonial Caribbean society assisted many women in 'bettering themselves' via education (Cooper and Davidson 1982; Ellis 1986). Unfortunately, some of their initial experiences led all but a few of these women into other employment.

But, despite these early disappointments, some women were able to gain access to training colleges and other further education institutions, and this finally led to employment in schools. Some women were also active in pioneering work setting up supplementary schools in their communities, working closely with religious organizations. Bryan, Dadzell and Scarfe (1985) cite the positive contribution of black women in the educational struggles of the 1960s and 1970s. The Rampton Committee (1981) acknowledged the role of supplementary schools. Other education commentators, such as Tomlinson (1984), also give an account of the 'Black-Education' movement during the last twenty years. This often served to provide the opportunities for some of the women who now hold management positions.

The importance of the home and the family – especially their mothers' encouragement in nurturing and supporting high ambitions – were recalled by two women:

> She felt that if you wanted to do anything you could do it in spite of the barriers.
>
> (A Senior Lecturer)

> Ambition comes from my mother, as I was raised by my mother. My father died when I was very young and she's always been somebody behind me, in front of me, pushing me, expecting me to do well, and there has always been a lot of encouragement from the home.
>
> (A Head of Department)

Encouragement from the home helped to compensate for lack of encouragement in the school system:

> I wasn't encouraged. Although I went to a very good school that had a very good academic reputation, I didn't feel I was encouraged at the time to achieve my full potential. It was almost as if the black girls [it was a girls' school] that were there were there in spite of themselves . . . quite a few of us did not come out with the academic qualifications that we should have done. I went on into teacher training, I remember, in a way in spite of my education – to actually show my teachers that I could amount to something. That was one of the first barriers. Then, when I got into teacher-training college, I wanted to become the kind of teacher that I thought I should be – a *black* teacher as opposed to a *teacher* – but I didn't feel that the teacher training I received

acknowledged that. There was absolutely nothing to do with black culture at all on the teacher-training programme. There was perhaps one module that lasted perhaps two or three weeks on race throughout the whole year, and that was it. We achieve in spite of the barriers that are set up.

(A Head of Department)

That interviewee also stressed the price required by 'good' schools and career 'success', and ways of avoiding the sacrifice of black identity:

For me, political awareness had to go alongside academic achieve-ment. It was important because I had actually seen what had happened to the few black girls that did succeed going to the good school I went to. It was as if to succeed they had to forfeit their own cultural background – that was the price of success. So I was, if you like, out to prove that you could do both. You could become academically successful, you could go on to a profes-sional career, and still maintain some sort of integrity towards your culture and working for your people. So I did a lot of reading that . . . had to do with my own cultural development. I didn't receive it in school, I didn't receive it in college; it was something I had to do off my own bat, and that has been a strong motivator towards helping me become the woman I am today.

(A Head of Department)

Most Headteachers depend to a great extent on the support and loyalty of staff. Black women felt that they often experienced more difficulty in being 'accepted' in this way. Part of the prob-lem might be understood if one recognizes that loyalty often comes out of shared values and/or cultural links. Consequently the 'hidden' values of the institution do not apply in the same way for black women in management. This in turn leads to isolation which is experienced to a greater degree than is the case for other women. There is an additional sense of separateness when one considers that a black Headteacher is likely to have only one or two, if any, black staff. Given that the role of the Headteacher usually creates isolation anyway, the additional stress can be appreciated. A similar situation also applies to black Heads of Department, who rarely have the experience of working with another black colleague.

Because of their isolation, it was felt that a democratic approach to management could help to break down some of the barriers. It was felt that, as black women, they brought particular strengths to management and decision-making. Having been subjected to various forms of oppression, they could understand how the other person might feel to be on the receiving end of action.

> I identify a type of management that females seem to practise more than males and that is they are people-oriented, they are people-centred. That does not mean that they are less skilful at their job or any less good at managing all sorts of things – time, people, whatever, or issues with tact – but they do seem to be able to listen to people, hear people and develop their organizations around the people that work within them . . . That would be the sort of management that I would prefer to pursue. It is the sort of style that I try to work in on a daily basis.
>
> (A Head of Unit)

This interviewee went on to describe how her way of managing provoked criticism from male colleagues:

> [They] see it as perhaps a little too spontaneous, too reactive. I prefer to run meetings . . . I realize there is a certain procedure that needs to be followed for meetings to be run effectively, but *people* are involved in meetings and sometimes you have to dispense with procedure. I feel that people should be heard and you can actually do things in a way where the majority of people can go away feeling comfortable, and I find that men do not like that – they'd much rather you stick to procedure and to hell with the people.
>
> (A Head of Unit)

The difficulty of implementing a female management style and the particular challenges for black women managers were also pointed out:

> You inherit situations and people who are used to working with different kinds of managers . . . It is very difficult for a black woman to change that and introduce discussions in her own style and culture. One of the things I try to do is make that acceptable to people. I also try to have all kinds of different forms of communication. I am quite flexible in the way that communications take place, and in that sort of way I am trying to create my own management style. Also in terms of who I involve . . . there has been a tendency to keep the community at a distance and only have meetings with certain managers in the system. Where possible I try to get community members involved in team meetings.

If not, I go out to meet them and try to act as a real link between the community and the service.

(A Head of Department)

Others talked about their management style – how they define it and put it into operation. This extract is representative:

I think it's about the way [women] are inclusive of other people and that we also act with a more integrated approach of feelings and objectivity, and that we use our intuition more. And of course common sense. I think we are far more egalitarian in our approach. It's probably because of our experience, which is much broader than men's . . .

People find it very difficult that I am wanting to include other people, I feel that decision-making isn't easy – it takes a long time and it isn't always the decision that we want. People find it difficult to accept that they are included as part of the decision-making process. But now it works really well, because they understand how we can work together. I've established the kind of management culture I want by demonstration – by demonstrating good practice, by bringing it to the forefront of any discussion in any scenario I am in. And getting other people to take it on board and see that it is an appropriate way of working whichever department you are in and whatever you are found with . . .

It leads to constant difficulties and conflicts, because white institutions are not used to including people – for instance, in my department, including workers in training in similar decision-making. Management is very hierarchical; it's not about democracy. I think my way of working brings conflict because it . . . raises issues about the way hierarchies make decisions and the process they use to ensure their authority and power is maintained. My way of working undermines that because it's far more person-centred. It's about people taking control.

(HMI)

Attempts at cooperative, community-linked and non-hierarchical styles of working were not without problems, however. There were occasions when even junior staff felt able to ignore requests or instructions. Because the management of people is an essential part of the job, the ongoing battles against negative attitudes were sometimes felt to undermine the self-confidence necessary in order to remain in 'control'.

We think about other people's feelings. Sometimes, though, this can cause problems because people think you are weak and can be manipulated. Women have more understanding and can find ways of working with other people, though as a black woman I find I have to constantly prove myself to both staff and parents.

(A Headteacher)

Black women are largely perceived by the wider society in a number of stereotyped ways, and this was put forward as a reason for some of the responses they received from staff and the wider community. Style of dress and hairstyle often cause unnecessary comments from both men and women. Sometimes these comments cause embarrassment, often leading to additional stress. The stereotyped view of black women as 'exotic' often seemed to encourage a certain amount of the 'disrespect'. For example, braided hair and traditional Asian dress often tended to be the focus of attention or discussion. It was felt that what was a normal part of a black woman's self-identity was treated as theatre.

Many education authorities identify themselves as equal-opportunities employers. Some even have well-developed policy statements on this. When asked about the impact of these policies on their careers, the interviewees' responses were mixed. One woman felt that equal opportunities policies had only a marginal effect:

I don't think equal opportunity policies are worth the paper they are printed on. I think you can say that because if you look across the service in which I work there are still no [women] seniors other than myself and no senior black women. On the other hand, I think you can use equal opportunities policies to get some of the things we want.

(A Departmental Course Manager)

While another was even more critical:

I found that equal opportunities policies have forced me to place gender and race against each other and forced me into a position where I have to choose between one and the other. Also, I found that, although I have been involved in authorities where they have very good-looking policy statements on paper, the actual slitting into practice and evaluating how effective those policies are have proved that the policies themselves don't actually work, because of the way they are implemented.

(A Head of Department)

The women interviewed mentioned their involvement in 'networking' in order to counter some of these experiences. This is a strategy which has been tried and found effective with other women in management. It is also a strategy which has quite a history in the black women's movement. Angela Davis (1982) gives an interesting account of the 'Club Movement', which became an important campaigning support network for black professional women. During the interviews, one woman talked about a group of fifteen black women in education who met regularly over a year:

> Well, obviously I needed to find women that I felt were in the same sort of situation – looking to develop themselves and at the same time who felt that they had a commitment to working for their community. From a very early stage in my career I joined black women's groups – not just for friendship and support, but also for very positive advice in terms of careers and the sorts of courses we ought to be looking to and general career development.
>
> A network of support is crucial – it is absolutely essential. I am working in a situation now with this authority where there is no immediate network of support around me, no women's group as such. So I keep in contact with women that I have known previously from other authorities. I think it is important that women learn not to work in isolation, whatever their job or whatever area they happen to be in: that they do have that network of support; that they develop themselves in such a way that they feel comfortable.
>
> (A Head of Unit)

Because of the sometimes daily encounter with racist and sexist attitudes, it became important that these women developed their own ways of handling such situations. Networking as adopted by this local group provided two points of action. First, the women gained the emotional support of other women who shared similar experiences. This was said to help the self-doubt that individual women often felt – 'Is it them or is it me?' The second benefit of networking was that it enabled the pooling of ideas and the sharing of tactics.

A very real question facing these women was a problematic one: how does anyone go about attempting to change an institution from within? In the light of their isolation and the stress that this caused, the task was viewed as daunting. The women who were Headteachers had a particular difficulty: their temptation was to adopt some of the characteristics associated with certain types of male management – for example, being aggressive or authoritarian. One Headteacher felt that she had used such methods on occasions, but this was greatly out of character.

Surprisingly, most of the women were quite positive in the action they took. They set out to identify 'allies' or any pockets of support and to work with these people. This served to build up a base from which to develop new ways of working or trying out new ideas. It was felt that schools and colleges were ideally placed to take on part of the responsibility for wider institutional change, and by doing so it would be possible to achieve genuine equality of opportunity.

The women who set out to adopt alternative management styles had varied experiences and degrees of success. Open management became possible, but only after some work had been done to raise awareness about the effects of racism and sexism. There are now many experienced black female trainers who are able to design programmes for any institution. Schools and colleges also have personnel who possess the skills to develop in-house staff-training courses which address the issues around black women's experiences.

On the whole these women gave the impression of being self-confident and in control. They wish to be regarded not as either 'victims' or 'superwomen', but as successful black women.

References

Bryan, A., Dadzell, F. and Scarfe, J. (1985) *Black Women's Lives in Britain*. London, Virago Press.

Cooper, R. and Davidson, H. (1982) *High Pressure: Working Lives of Women Managers*. London, Fontana.

Davis, Angela (1982) *Women, Race and Class*. London, The Women's Press.

Ellis, Pat (1986) *Women of the Caribbean*. London, Zed Books.

Rampton, Anthony (1981) *Interim Report of the Committee of Inquiry into the Education of Children from Ethnic Minority Groups*. London, HMSO.

Tomlinson, Sally (1984) *Home and School in Multicultural Britain*. London, Batsford.

CHAPTER 2

The Community Education Coordinator

Teaching is a career. On entering the job (I find it difficult to use the word 'profession' in this context), young teachers can see career pathways leading to a headship or perhaps even the dizzy height of Chief Education Officer. How is it, then, that so many women fail to pursue a unilinear career in the way that men do?

My own teaching experiences, which began in 1966, were prefaced by an education which was probably typical of that of thousands of capable girls of my era. In the hothouse atmosphere of a girls' grammar school, it was tacitly assumed that most pupils would progress to university or teacher-training college. Careers advice was non-existent, and those who did not aspire to higher education tended to find themselves marginalized by the school culture.

My particular interest – or rather fanaticism – was physical education. The PE teachers, who were gods to me, had all been trained at the same northern physical education college. So it was that I fell – or perhaps was pushed – into PE teaching as a career, and I attended the same college as my mentors.

My first teaching post, as a Scale-2 Head of Girls' physical education at a small, rural, mixed grammar school, came about when I was the only applicant and interviewee. The Headteacher was an autocratic, patriarchal, dry stick of a man who informed me, quite pleasantly, that the only important things girls needed to learn in physical education were hockey and tennis, so that they could play for the school teams and win – for the glory of the school. I felt constrained in my pedagogy, although in truth I did teach more or less what I wanted to – I just had to make sure that the school teams were successful. After four years in the school I felt so restricted that I looked around for any alternative job, even outside teaching.

My next appointment was to the staff of a primary school in a nearby town, where I taught upper juniors. Many of the children were massively disadvantaged, and the male Headteacher employed a most liberal approach to education. I went from a Scale-2 to a Scale-1 post at this time. I was happy to do so to maintain my interest in teaching, but my career was already beginning to zigzag.

All the classroom doors in this school were open, and the children were allowed to wander at will – in accordance with the Head's philosophy that children would be most motivated to learn if they had a choice of subject-matter. After some months in the school, I was offered a Scale-2 post, which I declined because I felt I had not had enough experience in the primary sector. I was also asked to apply for the deputy headship of a nearby school, but declined to do so for the same reason.

When the Headteacher of this, my second, school was appointed as an adviser in a neighbouring authority, he was replaced by a man who promptly closed all the classroom doors and changed the character of the school completely. I could not agree with him when he told us as a staff that, whatever home conditions the children lived in, these were not our concern in the classroom. It was perhaps fortunate that, when he had been at the school for two terms, I left to prepare for the birth of my first daughter.

For seven years I did not have a full-time job, as I stayed at home to bring up my young family. However, I was employed part-time in a variety of situations: as a physical-education teacher, as a swimming teacher, a housewives' sports coordinator at a leisure centre and as an evening adult education centre Principal. I also taught ante-natal classes for the National Childbirth Trust. All of this has subsequently been of no benefit to me in my career as it is not perceived to be relevant to the logical, hierarchical concept of career by the (mainly male) administrators in whose gift promotions are. I can say, however, that I benefited from widening my teaching experience, and I do feel quite strongly that the deeper understanding of child psychology which a mother who has spent time at home rearing her children inevitably has should actually profit her in her career.

When I resumed full-time teaching it was as a general teacher in the first-school department of a 5–12 primary school very close to my home. The need for me, as a mother with dual responsibilities – family and school – to take a job close to home caused me to make yet another detour in my career. (The term is beginning to sound a completely inappropriate one to describe my teaching experiences thus far.) The Head of this school was in his sixties. He was very traditional in his approach, but teachers were given absolute autonomy in their classrooms (a strategy which did nothing for the continuity of the pupils' education).

About a year after I went to the school, I was given a Scale-2 post for running an extra-curricular gymnastics club. This promotion restored the status I had had fifteen years previously in my first teaching post.

When I had been at the school for about two and a half years, the Head retired and the incoming Headteacher made sweeping changes in the school – many of which were long overdue. Before the new Head decided to train as a teacher, he had been in the armed forces. The school rapidly became more organized – not to say regimented – under his leadership. I agreed with many of the changes and with the more organized approach, and I worked willingly for the new Head initially. Numbers on roll were declining and, as Scale-3 teachers retired, their 'points' were withdrawn from the school. It is cold comfort to have been given the intimation that otherwise a Scale-3 post would have been mine.

Eighteen months after the arrival of the new Head, I started a three-year Open University Advanced Diploma in Education Management. Investigations into aspects of the school's management which I had to carry out as Open University assignments caused me some problems with the Head. In part this was because comments of the staff contained within these reports were mildly critical of the school or of the Head's management style, which I myself found to be somewhat autocratic. It was also noticeable that he was unwilling to delegate anything of significance.

At around this time, I had a number of interviews for deputy headships, but was not successful. The main feedback had suggested that I was too serious at interviews and in some cases that I was 'too strong' for the governors' liking.

I finished the Advanced Diploma in Education Management and went on to study for an Open University M.A. in Education. During the first year of this course (which was to take me two years) my relationship with the Headteacher was very bad, and I did, in fact, request a transfer from the school. With the help of the authority's Chief Adviser, I was seconded to another school in the borough to be a home–school liaison and community teacher. Written into the conditions of this secondment was the agreement that I would not go back to my previous school at the end of it.

This move represented complete liberation for me. I had the opportunity to put my ideology of community education into practice. I was also able to run in-service workshops on gender in education for advisers and teachers in the authority. I was given much of the responsibility which I wanted and felt more than ready for, but, as a result of changes in education legislation, I was back on a main-scale grade of pay – twenty-two years after qualifying as a teacher, with a broad spectrum of teaching experience behind me.

Towards the end of the secondment year I knew that I would have to make a decision about my future. The community network which I had initiated early in the school year had developed to such an extent that it was felt that a full-time coordinator was needed. As I had been responsible for setting it up, it was probably logical that I should do the job; but, with no firm assurance that the post would indeed materialize, I decided to apply for a post of advisory teacher within the authority which carried responsibility for gender in education. This was a Scale-D post. At this point, senior officers managed to identify funding to offer a network coordinator's post on a Scale-C allowance.

Obviously, either position represented a promotion for me, though not at the deputy-headship level to which I had previously aspired. I am extremely committed to tackling issues of gender in education, but I felt ownership of the community network project and finally decided not to apply for the advisory-teacher job. It is interesting to note that this post was subsequently withdrawn, and for a year I in fact did all the gender in-service training in the authority as well as my full-time job. I had to apply through the normal channels for the coordinator's post, although this turned out to be no more than a formality.

I have been working in this capacity for a year now. The project has a very high profile and is the subject of several national pilot projects, including one with the Open University.

The biggest challenge for me during the next year will be the coordination of the conversion of a (soon to be redundant) secondary school into a community base. This will, of course, include the identification of funding and a variety of user groups to make the initiative a viable proposition.

Perhaps, then, this is the zenith of my career. I have a very challenging, stimulating job which I have been allowed to develop according to my own instincts. My responsibility is now directly to Education Officers, as my remit covers five primary and two secondary schools. I have a clerical assistant who works with me, and I also have responsibility for deploying a part-time relief caretaker to facilitate out-of-hours community use of the schools.

I have absolutely no complaints about the job: it is substantially what I made it and is, as far as I know, a unique appointment, both in the way it was developed and also in the way it is funded (as well as the LEA, other council departments, the local health authority and the Church Urban Fund all contribute to my salary). Because of the unusual nature of the job, I am not sure what a logical career move for me would be, or whether, in fact, I have shunted myself into yet another siding. I do not quibble about remuneration for the job – I certainly understand the difficulties of funding a supernumerary post in the present economic climate. There are those in authority that I can talk to about the status of a Scale-C post, but this does not seem over-important to me at present. Within the authority, officers from several departments are talking about the network which has developed as a model which could – and perhaps should – be replicated in other areas of the borough.

In the final analysis, then, perhaps what I am saying is that I have found job satisfaction to be most important and I have rejected the unilinear, hierarchical concept of career as being inappropriate for me. There are a number of contributory factors to this. The first, I am sure, is situated within the personal realm, in that, when at any point in my career I encountered a management regime I fundamentally disagreed with, I would feel a need to move away from the situation. Had I known the culture of teaching better and had I been willing to become involved in the necessary micropolitical manœuvres, things might have been different. Another reason why the concept of 'career as ladder' is inappropriate for many women is the number of rungs which are removed if she takes time out to look after her family. The idea that a working mother will have a dual role – as homemaker as well as career woman – often strews more obstacles in her career pathway.

Hughes (1988: 18) describes teaching as a career 'that is essentially bureaucratic, in which teachers experience a succession of related jobs, arranged in a hierarchy of prestige, through which persons move in an ordered, predictable sequence'.

A number of commentators have described teaching as a series of stages. The first stage would cover the period between the ages of approximately twenty-one and twenty-eight. This is a time when teachers are likely to establish discipline, consolidate their subject specialisms and evolve their own personal style of pedagogy. I can identify with this stage, although I left teaching temporarily at the age of twenty-seven to start a family.

According to Sikes (1985: 44), the next stage occurs at around the age of thirty, when there is evidence of a greater sense of urgency. Sikes notes, however, that the differences between the sexes at this point can be quite considerable. Women teachers, at home with a young family, will be marking time, while the careers of their male ex-colleagues are gaining momentum.

The next phase, which occurs between the ages of thirty and forty, is again frequently experienced differently by men and women. Men can be seen to be establishing their place in society and to be working towards the peak of their careers. Many women re-enter teaching during this phase and often feel under pressure because, effectively, they have two jobs. I am sure it is true to say that, whether the questions are asked at interviews or not, many governors wonder whether women can handle increased responsibility at work, i.e. promotion, while at the same time running a home. This is not on the agenda for a man.

According to Miller *et al.* (1988: 19), 'The late thirties and early forties [are] a period of "questioning and cross-over" where women [become] more ambitious for leadership and management positions and men more family-centred and settled in their work.' As my children grew up and became more independent, I was able to give more time and consideration to my career. Many men, having had an uninterrupted run at their careers for some years, do ease off and give more time to their families.

Sikes (1985: 44) talks about the stage between the ages of forty and fifty-five where 'the major task for the age group . . . is coming to terms with and adapting to what can be seen as a plateau in the life career'. Women may not be ready to accept that 'promotion after forty grows increasingly unlikely' (Sikes 1985: 52), particularly if they feel a greater sense of freedom as their families become more independent. I have talked to several women, like me in their early forties, who have been unsuccessful at interview, and feedback from advisers has always included a reference to 'the problem of age'.

Anyone appointed to a headship at the age of forty-five could spend twenty years in the job. Women, liberated from family responsibilities, are often eager to channel their energies into their careers. In this situation, then, age is an irrelevance: the inability to undertake a management role in schools much after the age of forty is a construct of those in our society who lack the facility to treat people as individuals. Working mothers become the losers. 'The central issue is accepting and coming to terms with one's own mortality' (Sikes 1985: 52) – but so soon?

Teacher's careers are intimately bound up with their relationships with those in authority over them, particularly Headteachers. The leadership style which a Headteacher employs and the type of school he or she leads can have a profound effect upon the prospects of the staff in that school.

The male Headteachers and the one female Headteacher I have worked for employed very different leadership styles. Some of the male Headteachers adopted a managerial approach in which commanding, planning, coordination and control were notable features. Ball (1987: 97) opines that for such heads 'in theory at least, the roles and responsibilities of staff are relatively fixed and publicly recorded'. In one of the schools that I worked in, which had a male Head, staff let it be known that they felt that monitoring roles written into their job descriptions were impossible for full-time class teachers to carry out. The Head had to accept the fairness of such observations, but, I know, was not happy that this had been articulated, as it challenged the rationale on which the organization was founded.

Managerial heads are noted for their adherence to (or reliance on) bureaucratic, hierarchical systems. Ball (1987: 99) considers that 'it is possible and not uncommon to find the managerial head in the role of desk-bound bureaucrat' and that 'approaches to the head go through the proper channels, by the book'. Several of the male Heads of my acquaintance could be found, in normal circumstances, closeted in their offices, issuing written edicts and memoranda, often communicating with staff through the Deputy Head. Primary schools have notoriously flat hierarchies, but in such instances the apex of the pyramid is clearly visible. Such heads do indeed 'err . . . on the side of task function' and adhere to 'legal . . . rational procedures' (Ball 1987: 99). To them, staff may become as parts of the machine, to be slotted in so that the school operates smoothly.

In contrast, the female Head of my last school employs what Ball calls an interpersonal management style. She 'relies on personal relationships and face-to-face contact to fulfil [her] role' (1987: 87). Her door is always open (figuratively speaking at least), and there is a definite emphasis on ' "consideration", on the human function of the organization'. There is, of course, a formal hierarchy – the salary structure in schools decrees that this should be so – but communications do not have to flow through hierarchical channels. The Head actively canvasses the views of staff on a wide range of issues and will do so in the corridor, in the staff room or in the car park! And just as there is a formal hierarchy, so also is the school (like all schools to some extent) bureaucratic; but whereas the managerial Head is highly bureaucratized, relying on written forms of communication, for interpersonal heads 'talk is the work, i.e. it consumes most of an administrator's time and energy' (Gronn 1988: 291). A study by Lester Davies (1987: 44) revealed that when Heads were studied for a week, 'an average of thirty-four hours was spent in verbal contact: this accounted for eighty-three per cent of the head's total work commitment'. I have seen the female Head that I worked for acquire significant resources and other advantages for her school through her facility to communicate verbally. This brings me to a very important difference between the two leadership styles. For interpersonal heads, '. . . the school is the person' (Ball 1987: 91), but for managerial heads, '. . . the system of organization as such is separate from the headteacher as a person' (Ball 1987:98). It will be interesting to relate this to gender issues later in the chapter.

There is a close co-relation between the sort of managerial leadership style I have described and machine bureaucracy as an organizational form which there is no space in this chapter to pursue. Both, however, are rigid and inflexible and make it difficult for a school to institute change without significant upheaval. In contrast, the female Head I have described, with her interpersonal leadership style, leads an organization which has the flexibility to respond to its environment and to the recent legislative measures imposed by central government.

The thrust of the current government's educational legislation lends itself naturally to the managerial style of leadership. It is also masculine in its orientation. 'Weber saw the increasing subdivision of work as part of a universal process of rationalization in which jobs were systematically ordered, routinized and subjected to centralized management control' (Ozga and Westoby 1988: 46). He went on to suggest that the growth of bureaucracy, with its control mechanisms '. . . to ensure behaviour conformant with the rational plan of the organization' (p. 46) typified the concept of the universal process of rationalization. Morgan (1986: 178) considered the '. . . links between the male stereotype and the values that dominate many ideas about the nature of organization . . . organizations are often encouraged to be rational, analytical, strategic, decision-oriented, tough and aggressive and so are men'. Central government is trying to impose a rational, bureaucratic system on schools, much in line with the working practices of male, managerial Heads. The prognosis for the future might be more hopeful if administration were to become known less as an essentially rational process and more as '. . . the product of chaotic conditions and a great deal of struggle and ambiguity' (Hoyle 1988:225). In my experience, female Heads are more likely to possess the flexibility and interpersonal skills to face up to the realities of this situation.

According to Morgan (1986), men are logical, rational, aggressive, exploitative, strategic, independent and competitive. They are also considered to be leaders and decision-makers. The male Heads I have described in this chapter would recognize this view of themselves. Morgan sees women as intuitive, emotional, submissive, empathic, spontaneous, nurturing and cooperative. Under no circumstances could the female Head I have worked for be described as submissive, and I certainly do not see her in the role of 'loyal supporter and follower' (Morgan 1986: 179), but otherwise the characteristics correspond.

As Arnot says (in Arnot and Weiner 1987: 115), 'boys are trained to . . . make the distinction between work and non-work, masculinity and non-masculinity . . . Their masculinity is premised upon maintaining the distinctiveness of the two spheres, since it is in that hierarchy that their power is based'.

As previously mentioned, for the female Head 'the school is

the person' (Ball 1987: 91), whereas for the male Heads of my acquaintance 'the system of organization as such is separate from the Headteacher as a person' (Ball 1987: 98). This makes it much easier for these male Heads to avoid taking personal responsibility for failure.

The managerial leadership style is hierarchical in its orientation. It is significant, then, that 'men tend to see their aspirations in a narrow hierarchical sense – the career as ladder' (Ozga and Westoby 1988: 19) whereas women have 'a rather negative attitude to hierarchy' (Ball 1987: 74), moving sideways as well as upwards. My present community post is exciting and challenging, but was to all intents and purposes a sideways move. One of the male Headteachers I worked for climbed the career ladder from probationer to Headteacher in seven short years. The female Headteacher described in this chapter, on returning to teaching after having a family, experienced considerable difficulty in acquiring a headship.

I consider it to be an incontrovertible truth, then, 'that gender is immensely important in the selection of the style of management, and in shaping relations between head, deputy and other staff' (Ozga and Westoby 1988: 14). All of my personal experience tends to support this statement.

So, what of the future? The country is in a period of great social and economic change, and schools have many new challenges to face up to. As Blumer says (1987: 83), 'the essence of organization lies in an on-going process of action – not in a posited structure of relations'. The evidence would suggest that, on the whole, female Heads are better placed to face up to the challenge. What a pity there are not more of them!

References

Arnott, M. and Weiner, G. (1987) Gender and Education, E813 Study Guide. Milton Keynes, OUEE.

Ball, S. J. (ed.) (1987) *The Micropolitics of School: Towards a Theory of School Organization*. London, Methuen.

Blumer, J. (1987) in S. J. Ball (ed.) *The Micropolitics of School: Towards a Theory of School Organization*. London, Methuen.

Davies, L. (1987) *Educational Management and Administration*, 43–7.

Gronn, P. C. (1988) 'Talk as the work: the accomplishment of school administration' in A. Westoby (ed.) *Culture and Power in Educational Organizations*. Milton Keynes, Open University Press.

Hoyle, E. (1988) 'Micropolitics of educational organizations' in A. Westoby (ed.) *Culture and Power in Educational Organizations*. Milton Keynes, Open University Press.

Hughes, E. (1988) 'Institutional office and the person' in J. Ozga and A. Westoby *Educational Organizations and Professionals*, E814 Study Guide. Milton Keynes, OUEE.

Miller, J., Taylor, G. and Walker, K. (1988) *Teachers in Transition: The Study of an Ageing Teaching Force*. Ontario, OISE.

Morgan, G. (1986) *Images of Organization*. Beverley Hills, Sage Publications.

Ozga, J. and Westoby, A. (1988) *Educational Organizations and Professionals*, E814 Study Guide. Milton Keynes, OUEE.

Sikes, P. (1985) 'The Life cycle of the teacher' in S. Ball and I. Goodson (eds) *Teachers' Lives and Careers*. Lewes, Falmer.

CHAPTER 3

The Chief Education Officer

A Conversation with MARGARET MADEN

Margaret Maden is one of the few women Chief Education Offi-cers. In the 1990s, more appeared, especially in the London boroughs which were formerly part of the ILEA. More women have been moving into educational administration at more senior levels, but they are still underrepresented in senior positions. Recently the professional body of educational administrators, the Society of Education Officers, was criticized for its failure to promote equal opportunities in the areas of race and gender.

Margaret Maden was dealing with the consequences of the introduction of the Education Reform Act when I approached her about contributing to this book, and she felt that the best way in which she could be included was through recording a conversa-tion. The extracts from that conversation which follow cover a number of themes which are central to this book: the 'career' route, female management styles, and strategies for encouraging equal opportunities.

The career route

M.M. I started in education administration in 1986, when I was seconded from being Director of the Islington Sixth Form Centre in the ILEA, to be Principal Adviser for the develop-ment of tertiary education in the ILEA. I worked there for a year, and during that year I felt that I wanted to continue in education administration but not necessarily in the ILEA, so I applied for the Deputy CEO's job here in Warwickshire and was appointed. I started in October 1987 and then I was appointed to being CEO the following summer and took up that appointment this January, 1989.

My career started in the ILEA – or, as it was then, the LCC – in 1962, as an Assistant Teacher in a comprehensive school in Brixton and then, after four years, I moved into a college of education for mature students and I was there for almost five years. Then I moved to being Deputy Head of a comprehensive school in Oxfordshire, and after four years I moved back to London to be Head of a comprehensive school in Islington. From there, after eight years, I went to be Director of this new Islington Sixth Form Centre. So that is an unusual route. At the time I was moving into education administration in Warwickshire there was an understanding that, because of the Education Reform Act, which was then still a Bill, the role of the education authority and of the CEO was changing and more emphasis was placed on first-hand experience of what it was like to be in a school or an institution rather than in administration. So I think really I just came along at the right time.

J.O. When you were in schools, could you tell me a little about how you moved up through the hierarchy? Was it fairly rapid? It must have been, and why do you think it was? Were you fairly ambitious when you went into teaching as a career – did you see it as a career?

M.M. No I didn't. I think, like a lot of women, I've never had a career plan. I know women, and indeed men, now are advised to – you know, 'think ahead' and all of that. I've never done that. I think it was quite interesting that after my first job in Brixton, after two years, I was promoted there to what was then Scale 2 – still quite modest. I was never a Head of Department or anything like that, which is the sort of standard route through and up, and I actually took a pay cut in order to go and work in the college of education with mature students, because I was just very interested in that and I felt that it would teach me quite a lot – which it did – as well as hoping to do something about teacher training, which at that stage I was beginning to get very interested in. I could have well stayed in teacher training except that towards the third or fourth year in that college I was beginning to get itchy feet and thinking I want to get back into schools, and it was considered quite unusual that I would go back into a deputy headship of a very big comprehensive school in Oxfordshire.

Now I have to say at that point that I was invited to apply for that job by somebody who'd heard me speak at a conference – probably an NUT conference or some pressure group, because I was always very active, not only in the NUT but also in pressure groups to do with the reform of teacher training and comprehensive education and I always kept on writing articles for journals or chapters for books – this kind of thing. So I think that early stage of not concentrating simply on my paid employment but also taking a very broad interest and being actively involved in education outside the establishment I was working in – in pressure groups or in the NUT – was actually very important in terms of my career. So I was invited to apply for the job in Bicester, in Oxfordshire, by the Head, and it was in those days when the way the Head advised the governors more or less settled it, although I do remember being interviewed alongside other candidates and being asked – and I was then aged twenty-nine – did I really think I was strong enough to take on a job like this and didn't I think it was quite possible that I might suddenly go off and get married and have children. That was clearly stated as unarguable as a reason why I shouldn't take on a job of that kind. But anyhow I think the Head's advice prevailed and I was appointed.

J.O. How did you respond to that question, can you remember?

M.M. I think – I can't remember very clearly – I wasn't conscious in the way one would be nowadays that it was a sexist question, because this was 1969 and on the whole that kind of thinking was prevalent, but I remember being slightly stunned in the sense that I wasn't sure quite how to reply and as far as I recall I said something along the lines of, well, I think I wouldn't be applying for this job unless I had thought about all of that. I can think of better answers now, but that was my response at the time. I had, two or three months before that interview, applied under my own steam as it were for a deputy headship in Hertfordshire, in a Hertfordshire comprehensive, and there I was told by the Head afterwards, and the Divisional Officer, that they thought I was probably very good quality but they really needed the strength of a man for that post. Again I was rather stunned and I didn't know quite what to make of that, except I felt very insulted, because I thought even then I was stronger than many men I knew. And I think there's no doubt about it that not being married and not having children has made my career development much easier. I'm very aware of how remarkable it is that women manage – occasionally anyhow – to combine marriage and child-rearing with career development, but that was never anything I was very interested in. And I learnt a lot at Bicester as a Deputy Head, and there was quite a bitter experience there of men thinking it was rather strange that I was not going to be the classic Senior Mistress, which was the previous holder's role in that school – that the Head of the school was quite clear he didn't want the kind of classic Senior Mistress who arranged flowers and made the coffee and all of that.

J.O. They thought you should be dealing with 'girls' problems'?

M.M. Yes. When I was clearing out the filing cabinet, as I was moving into my predecessor's office, the bottom drawer was entirely full of Tampax, and part of her job had been to hand out Tampax to girls who needed it. Well, I don't recall having done that particular job. I don't know what the girls who used Tampax did after I didn't do that. But I was much more involved in curriculum planning and timetabling and innovations of one sort or another, and it was very exciting and a very good period, and a very good school. After four or five years, somebody I knew – again on the administration – said to me that there was a school he was a governor of in Islington that was in real trouble and would I be interested in applying for the headship. Again, I was asked to apply for something – I didn't do it on my own.

J.O. You're talking about sponsorship, which is fairly common in male careers and possibly more difficult for women. Men tend to sponsor one another. It's easier for them to meet socially and to build up good networks, but you did it by entering into that arena, didn't you, through conferences, through outside connections?

M.M. I think there was a certain advantage because I was seen to be a young woman, and I suppose the fact that I seemed to be then relatively attractive and, you know, well-dressed, stylish, all of that, was in a way . . . I mean, I think there was a sexual element in there, that men found this very intriguing. That is something that I think is unfair and wrong, but none the less I'm quite sure, looking back on it, that was a factor of my standing out in conferences, because I could string more than a few words together. I wasn't stupid, but at the same time the fact that I was a reasonably attractive female brought another element into it.

J.O. Were you surprised when you were appointed here? Did you come here thinking that when you applied for the Deputy's job it might be a route into being Director?

M.M. The advertisement made it clear that they were looking for somebody who saw themselves in a few years as a Chief Education Officer – either in Warwickshire, because it was known then that the CEO was going to retire within the next few years, or elsewhere – and I thought, because then I was forty-six, that I didn't see myself as staying as a Deputy – by then I'd got used to the idea of 'being in charge', but, you know, that's another illusion. So I was interested. I thought, having been appointed as a Head of a London comprehensive at the age of just coming up to thirty-five, which was then very young, and I headed that school and then opened up the Islington Sixth Form Centre, that I ought to move fairly quickly, and in fact the Warwickshire job was the first job, except for my very first job, that I really applied for on my own without being invited or anybody knowing me at this end, and when I came here for the interview I was the only woman amongst the candidates.

The sitting tenant, Martin Davis, who is now Director of the National Curriculum Council, had just got the job to be CEO in Newcastle on Tyne, and he said to me, 'Well, I think you're a very interesting candidate, but you're certainly not Warwick-shire. But, anyhow, it'll be good experience for you.' I felt quite miffed at this, because I thought I'm not used to being treated like this, and maybe that did me some good in my interview – I don't know. It was very interesting – I didn't like the feel of Warwickshire on the first day of interviews, when I met senior officers: I thought it was all rather stodgy, and I didn't see that I could actually do a very effective job here, because there seemed to be no sense of the need to change or to be flexible. But on the second day there were interviews by elected members and it was then a hung council, so we had the three parties represented and I felt much better about Warwickshire, because there seemed to be a sense of energy and commitment to change and flexibility, so I stayed and in fact I was appointed – although two of the Conservative members walked out when it was clear that I was being appointed. I think what they were most concerned about – well, equally – was that I was a woman and that I was from the ILEA, which was a kind of double jeopardy.

J.O. You must have really done well to have got the appointment, given that there must have been both inertia and a fair amount of conservatism about appointing a woman.

M.M. I think I concentrated on the fact in my interview and in my application that the kind of experience I'd had in London demonstrated that I was able to turn round situations from being ones of relative failure and uncertainty into successes, and that I knew quite a lot about the quality of education – the council was beginning then to get very concerned about being clearer about quality and raising standards. Now I think some prejudice existed against me because I was from the ILEA, where there is a reputation of low standards – rightly or wrongly – but I think my track record was very much about jacking things up and improving standards and improving the public credibility of two institutions in one of the most difficult parts of London. I had also that one year's experience in the ILEA's administration, and I was able at least to reflect upon what I'd learned there in a way that I think was reasonably convincing.

Management style

J.O. How did you find out how educational administration worked and, more specifically, how Warwickshire worked – its culture, the procedures and so on? Were you socialized into it at all?

M.M. No, not at all. It doesn't matter too much now, because the Education Reform Act is changing so fundamentally the relationship between the local authority and the school or the college, that we're all learning, whether we've been in education administration for donkey's years or not. I still find educational administration – I found this in the ILEA, and I find it here – more hierarchical than schools or colleges, with a tendency to be more rigid, and I think probably that one of the qualities that women often bring to management jobs is the capacity to be more flexible and to often think in a more divergent way and to compromise. Those can often be bad features, but I think in management frequently they're good features – a good characteristic. I think some of that is to do with women's domestic role, and I think this is learned from a very, very early age.

The extent to which women have to, or do, think about several things at different levels at the same time – perform functions both extremely humble and high-level management at the same time – actually builds up a kind of operational flexibility which is very important in modern management, and I think this applies to – well, virtually to all women, and carries on being important. That's why married women with children are quite remarkable if they manage to work through a career, because everything's against them, but all that ability to juggle several different-size balls in the air at the same time is actually something that's built in – that on the one hand we think is unfair and wrong but on the other hand certainly does strengthen the kind of managerial muscle or potential that women have. I know even as a single woman, when I work a fifteen- or sixteen-hour day and I'm sitting in a governor's meeting or some other committee, at seven, or eight, or nine in the evening, that I have to make sure that I've got a meal that I can make when I go home and that if the water board needs to come in – you know, all of those domestic things. Women have to do all of that as well as their jobs. On the whole men don't, and they've got a much simpler, linear, view of their careers and their lives than women – and I think they're the worse for it, actually. Even though women complain – and understandably, because the burden is too much in many cases – that they have to do all these different things at once, none the less I think there are benefits that accrue.

J.O. Do you remember developing any particular strategies for dealing with the fact that you were a woman in contexts where most of the other managers were men? Did you have ways of dealing with meetings, for example, or did the way in which you handled it simply come naturally?

M.M. No, I don't think any of this came naturally. I probably went over the top if anything on being seen to be knowledge-able and intellectual and analytical, and I think that led to a lot of men always describing me as formidable and actually being rather frightened of me – not knowing what to make of this curious phenomenon. It's only really in the last ten years or so that, relatively speaking, I've eased up on that, although I know I haven't cast off that image totally, because still people say that they find me very formidable. I don't think they would if I was a man: I think it's because I'm a woman and that I appear to be analytical and knowledgeable and rational – that is something of a surprise, and also something of a threat.

J.O. Have you encountered a lot of opposition – especially now, where you're a woman managing men? Have you developed ways of dealing with that?

M.M. I think I worried for a time about techniques and strategies to win people over, and then I got so involved in the task that I thought, well, damn it, I'm just going to concentrate on what I think is important and hope that people come along with me. At the same time, I have to say that I find no difficulty – quite the reverse – in listening to people. I think again this may be a slightly more female characteristic, that women on the whole are good listeners and that, while that can become very passive, I think it's quite important in my case that people on the whole do seem to realize that I do listen but at the same time that I'm pretty decisive. I'm not sure why I am, actually – that's what other people tell me: they see me as being very decisive. No, I think you just have to – this sounds rather inadequate – but I think you just have to maintain your own integrity and be yourself, as long as that self is actually recognized as genuine and concerned with the job. In a sense, I got away with murder with staff when I was Head of this rather difficult school in ILEA, in terms of what I was expecting them to do and expecting them to change into, because it was finally recognized that I had the best interests of the school at heart, and that actually matters – things like that do matter. So I haven't got any well-worked-out system of how to win hearts and minds, except really to get on with the job, I'm afraid.

J.O. But behind that there's a fair amount of confidence, isn't there, in your capacity to do that job, and this is often an area where women have difficulties – even if they know that they're good at a job, they don't go around giving the impression of being good at a job. It seems to me they're more often likely to express reservations about their capacities in a self-critical way, which men tend not to do – though they may have the same worries, they don't express them. Do you think you were

naturally confident from fairly early on in your career, or was
it something that you developed because you did things and
you were successful?

M.M. I think it builds up. Obviously the more one can establish
success incrementally – sometimes quite modest, but none the
less building up like a series of building blocks – the more confidence develops. A lot of that is to do with how far other
people say you're successful. I think one of the things that more
senior management jobs carry with them is less and less overt
feedback about success or otherwise – the signs are tacit rather
than overt or explicit. I was like most women, I guess, because
I was never prepared to believe for a long time that if I was
apparently successful or invited to join a committee or a working party that it wasn't simply because I was a young woman. I
think that's why I kept moving on – this business of proving to
myself that I was intellectually able and all of that sort of stuff.

When I went to university from school, I was discouraged
quite actively by my school in applying for university, because
they said I wasn't good enough. I actually got into university
not because of the formal interview but because of a quite
random, accidental meeting with the Head of the Department
as I came out of the interview and he was so amazed at seeing
this apparition in formal school uniform – grey suit and fedora
hat and all the works – that he said afterwards, 'Well, I just
decided you had to join the department,' and so he reversed the
decision that had just been made that I shouldn't be accepted. I
went on for a long time thinking, well, actually my problem is
that I'm just basically very stupid and I've just got to keep on
working up this grey matter, because it's obviously rather defi-
cient. But at the same time I'd always been encouraged at
home, to be fair, by my father and mother to enter into arguments with my elder brother.

Promoting equal opportunities

J.O. Do you think you've done anything in your present post –
are there any concrete, specific things that you feel that you
could do – to encourage more women to follow your example?

M.M. Appoint them.

J.O. Is it as easy as that?

M.M. It's quite easy, actually. I've always found it easy. I was quite amazed when I came here to see that there were no women at Chief Officer, Deputy Chief Officer or senior level – I mean just none, and I'm not just talking about education here.

J.O. But that would be standard for this kind of authority.

M.M. Well, maybe, yes.

J.O. Rather different from ILEA.

M.M. Well, yes, that's true. I failed to appreciate that in ILEA – partly because it's the capital city but also in part because of the policies there – there were so many women in senior positions in schools, colleges and in the authority itself. I'd just taken that as normal, and of course it's not normal. But here I've spent a fair bit of time encouraging women in the education department to go on training courses. Wherever I've worked, when setting up a working party of a committee or a study group, I've consciously involved women – not just for the sake of it but to think about the women in the department who have potential and to give them an opportunity to get into a broader area of work and operation. If I'm chairing a meeting, or even if I'm not, and there's a particular woman who's there and not saying anything, which is quite often the case, I'll ask for her views. I think we have to use every kind of device, and in three or four administrative posts and in about nine or ten inspectorate posts in the last year or eighteen months we've appointed women, and I think that that has really come down to my making sure, not in any kind of heavy way, that on the agenda at the shortlisting stage there is a consideration of looking at the women's applications, if there are any, just a little more carefully. Because there is also that ageism that enters in about women who've taken out a few years for child-rearing, and sometimes it is tempting for men, and sometimes women, to say, 'oh well, they're over the top' or 'they've missed out on a key stage of their career,' and all of that. But I think that even in education administration – certainly in these inspectorate appointments – there are plenty of able women around, and they are applying. I think things are getting better in education administration. Some of my colleagues think it's because of the woman CEO that more women now are applying, although we haven't any data to compare what it was like.

J.O. I would have thought that was quite likely.

M.M. Possibly – I don't know. On the schools side, very early on – when I came here as Deputy – I was involved in a week-end conference on equal opportunities for teachers and some figures were presented there about how many women there were in the authority's schools in various senior positions, and the position was virtually none. I was really very shocked, and I have encouraged some of my male colleagues to take the lead. in equal opportunities, because I don't think it would be entirely a good thing in Warwickshire if I was seen to be leading too much on this – although I think everybody's aware that I'm very aware of all these issues. And we've had secondments of two women teachers to conduct a survey into the opportunities for women teachers in secondary schools in Warwickshire, and we've now followed that with a similar survey into primary schools. And we've had a very successful course for middle managers from schools – women – for promotion. We've given them practice in applying for jobs, and interviews, videos – all of that kind of fairly practical workshop approach – and out of the thirty-nine Heads in Warwickshire secondary schools we now have six women. When I first came here it was three, so I suppose that's some improvement. So there is more of an awareness, and I think in Warwickshire that's very important, actually. I don't think the kind of ILEA approach of having endless turgid statements and documents and glossy brochures would go down at all well in Warwickshire.

J.O. If that heavy-handed, top-down approach doesn't work here, what does?

M.M. Well, for example, when I got here there was a small group of advisers who had taken upon themselves the review of equal opportunities in schools and they'd already produced a little pamphlet – quite low-key but actually rather good – that was largely to do with considering how teachers taught: about how much time was spent in attending to girls in the class as opposed to boys and all sorts of hidden curriculum messages in schools, and in that way raising awareness among staff who I would have thought hitherto had not given much thought to these sorts of issues at all. Similarly our multicultural policy takes the same kind of line – in other words, not hitting people over the head with how wicked they are but saying, 'Look – I think there are certain things you ought to just think about,' and also some light monitoring of outcomes and practices and processes in schools, undertaken by the advisers.

J.O. What are the prospects for equal opportunities within educational administration, within the directorate? Is there any sign of change within the Society of Education Officers, within the group as a professional body?

M.M. I think there were fairly stiff, predictable reactions two or three years ago when certain – very, very few – women in the SEO made a case out to the SEO for more attention to be paid to the needs of women and the need to promote and encourage women. I think that that's now moved on to a better stage because there are now men on the SEO executive who do not see it as at all threatening or unusual but in fact quite welcome a more broadly based executive and working parties and committees – broadly based in the sense of men and women but also ethnic minorities, who amazingly are now coming through into education administration, you know, because it is actually easier for women to make movements than it is for ethnic minorities, which I think women ought to remember from time to time, and I think there is a strong networking.

I think it's amazing that even in my time I'm part of a kind of change – partly because of the appointment of Directors of Education to the new inner-London boroughs, where I think half are women, but also quite apart from that I think there are now eight or nine women CEOs whereas I think when I came in here as Deputy there were only two or three. So I know it's still very, very limited, relatively, but it is moving and at the same time you've got to look right across the education profession. There are women in key jobs in the polytechnics. I don't think we've got there, but I think one shouldn't underestimate the progress that has been made over the last few years. I think we're now into another phase where, because of the desperate search for skills and the complete turn around in a lot of managerial, executive jobs of there being a shortage of labour rather than too much, women will now benefit for those more pragmatic reasons. There is now that shift from the more idealistic reason for promoting equal opportunities, which is to do with justice and fairness, into the more pragmatic – to saying. 'My God, we've got to find everybody who is skilled labour, even if it's a woman.' I think we should be quite clear about the strength of the pragmatic reasons behind promoting women.

CHAPTER 4

The Secondary Head

A Conversation with MAUREEN SEDGWICK

This chapter takes the form of a conversation with the Head of a 1,300-pupil comprehensive on the outskirts of Bristol. Maureen Sedgwick is a very experienced Headteacher, now in her third headship, who manages to run her school and also to play an active part in the local educational community – as a national union officer and a member of the local CATE committee. She is also a magistrate. In her career in education she has been part of many considerable changes in every aspect of schooling, and has also witnessed – and been part of – changes in the attitudes to women in senior posts. She came from a background which gave her confidence in her capacity and inculcated in her a lifelong habit of development and extension of that capacity. She is also of that generation of capable women who made a 'choice' to pursue her career rather than attempt the combination of career, marriage and family which creates the current 'double burden'. Her reflections on the difficulties faced by the next generation of women managers make interesting reading, as indeed does her account of her career in education.

We started with her family background. I asked her how she came to be in teaching:

M.S. I came along what used to be a very traditional route. From my small village school I went on to an all-girls convent school and then continued into higher education. It was a predictable choice: teaching was one of the few professions which girls were expected to follow, so I did. My mother was a lecturer in education, and there were teachers in my father's family, too, although he was an engineer. So, a general interest in teaching was evident on both sides of the family.

J.O. Was teaching something you wanted to do as well as something that was expected of you?

M.S. Not really. I enjoyed being in school – the prospect of continuing in that environment was attractive. I love books and I love being with people. Very simply, I like the ambience of school. I was drawn to teaching, but in many ways it wasn't a consciously thought-out decision that this was my vocation in life – it was just that so many of my friends were saying 'Well, what are you going to do?' and it was either teaching or the civil service or, if you were a very high flyer, medical school.

J.O. Can you tell me about your training?

M.S. Initially my training was at Liverpool. However, I have continued with further academic and professional studies throughout my career. I have taken two years out – secondment – one to do a specialist teaching-of-English course and another to obtain a master's degree at Sussex. Also, I have undertaken numerous long-term courses – evening and weekends – to acquire greater expertise and qualifications. For example, in educational management – Diploma – law – LL.B. degree – Teacher Librarian Certificate, secondary education – advanced diploma – Cambridge TEFL and in youth leadership.

J.O. What was the extent of your initial experience in teaching English before you were promoted?

M.S. When I started, I was a general-subjects teacher with a specialism in English. This was a mixed secondary school, and I taught 'O' level examination classes in English Language and English Literature. From there, I went to a girls' secondary school as Head of English. This was selective at age thirteen, so pupils who had missed out on the eleven-plus were afforded a second bite of the cherry. I taught 'O' level Language, Literature, Greek and Roman Literature in translation and RE. Then I went to Bradford, a bilateral school, which had more boys than girls – many more boys than girls – about two-thirds of the school. I held a joint appointment there – Head of English and that which was termed 'Lady Housemaster'. As you would imagine, most of my colleagues were men. Later, I went to Hertfordshire as Deputy Head. This school was starting from scratch with a first-year intake only, of about seventy pupils in new, purpose-built accommodation. It was our responsibility to build up the school. So I did lots of other things as well as the usual Deputy Head tasks – I was Head of English, Librarian and theatrical producer. During my seven years there, I continued with these responsibilities and taught English to pupils of all abilities and all ages, including examination classes at 'O' and 'A' level.

As a Head, I believe that direct teaching contact with pupils is valuable, so I have tried to keep some English teaching. However, reluctantly, I gave it up in 1988, because a regular, daily, timetabled commitment was incompatible with the increasing number of administrative and managerial responsibilities of a Head. Nowadays, I teach GCSE Law to year-12 pupils – they are old enough to get on with their work if I am called out of class.

J.O Do you feel that it was an advantage in being an English teacher in terms of being considered for promotion?

M.S. Yes I do. In fact I have had two major advantages in my career. English, certainly. I like meeting people, perhaps because of acting and debating. I enjoy interviews also, which may be masochistic, but it's interesting to anticipate the topics which might come up in an interview. I've usually got three or four alternative approaches to any problem, so, if one doesn't work then I have another one to hand. To say I enjoy a challenge sounds trite, because these days just about everything is a challenge. However, I find it stimulating to pit my wits against those of others in a given situation. English has been an advantage to me – all my career moves, before I got my first headship – were within my subject area. I had done a great deal of GCE examining, too, in Language and in Literature.

Another really important factor is that all my own teachers had been women. I had females as role models all the time I was growing up. We girls were never put down; we were encouraged to contribute to a wide range of activities. It was just the same at home; all our fathers were in the forces – Second World War – so our mothers ruled the roosts. These circumstances made it a matriarchal society.

One of the things I must say is that I have seldom felt I was competing *as a women* against men. I have competed in many situations with other professional people, but I've never felt disadvantaged because I am a woman. I don't think I've gone the other way, either, and tried to capitalize on being female. Until fairly recently – say the last ten years – it hadn't occurred to me that feminism was an issue. I know that might seem ridiculous, but it's because my own experiences had not caused me to think differently.

J.O. Are you saying in effect that it didn't occur to you as an issue because you never encountered any particular gender-related forms of prejudice or discrimination or difficulty? Or do you think you didn't perceive them?

M.S. I probably didn't perceive them at all. Apart from one school, all my experiences as a teacher have been in mixed schools, and I have been either extremely blinkered or extremely fortunate because I genuinely don't recollect feeling 'Well, I am not going to be able to do that because I'm a woman.' For example, in my first teaching job the previous Head had retired, and instead of promoting an existing member of staff – which would have been the usual pattern at that time – the governors had actually gone trawling for somebody with a bit of 'get up and go'. The new Head and I got on extremely well, because he wanted to introduce Music and Drama. I was very enthusiastic and was able to give a fair amount of time, after school, to doing these activities with children and parents and also with former pupils who still wanted to be connected to the school. The only time when I had what, in retrospect, I would call a tricky period was when I went to Bradford as Head of English and 'Lady Housemaster'. It was obvious that some of the staff there, which was very largely male, seemed to be trying to make life a little bit difficult, but I assumed they were testing me, as a young teacher, to see what I could do. However, I was certain that I could do the jobs, so I had no worries. The allocation of staff to the houses was determined by a male Deputy Head. When I checked on the people in my team, I found a lot of them would be regarded as weaker members of staff, quite a few probationers and one unqualified teacher. There was a lot of absenteeism. It did occur to me as a newcomer that I had been given a fairly mixed bunch to see how I could cope.

J.O. And how did you cope?

M.S. Well, I just did. I tried to do things with people, rather than to say 'Why didn't you do so and so?' I talked to colleagues, asked them to come and share problems with me and to work together for solutions. It's a long time ago now, but I've always tried to provide support when faced with such problems, rather than tell people they're inadequate. It seems to me to be the most practical way of going about things. It could have been, I suppose, a difficult time for me, but in fact it turned out not to be so. We had all sorts of activities at lunch-times – inter-house competitions, which I was enthusiastic about. Colleagues assumed that my house might be encouraged by me to participate in debates and things of that sort. They didn't think I would be quite so keen on cheering on the five-a-side, but of course I loved it. You see, I would be there cheering everybody on, and also, of course, encouraging the tutors and other pupils to do the same – which they did. It was very much a question of saying 'Let's all do it together.' That seemed to work.

J.O. Do you think you intimidated people?

M.S. I don't think they knew what to make of me. I have been happy and fortunate in my own schooling and in the people I have known. I like children, and I know that most of those I have taught have responded positively to me. I have that sense of security which comes from knowing that I can do my job.

All of my promotions have meant a change of school, so I am used to being an outsider. When I came here, many of the teachers had been on the staff from the day the school was established, in 1957. I knew that they would have reservations about somebody new anyway, but I was different from my male predecessor – I was female, and much younger. An exception to that was when I went to Stevenage as Deputy Head. The Head there was marvellous. He hadn't been a Deputy – he'd been Head of Modern Languages, but he'd applied for the headship and got it. He particularly wanted a young Deputy Head, one who was prepared to turn a hand to anything. He was most generous – he shared everything with me, and that gave me the basis for learning how to go about consultation and to get cooperation, because he did it and I followed his example. I learned everything about headship from him – an opportunity which not many Deputy Heads have. So, those experiences, self-confidence and a gregarious nature have helped me to take things on. I find most people I meet are helpful, interesting and non-threatening. That has been my experience since I was a little girl. Consequently, whenever I've found myself in a new situation I have had no reason to suppose that there might be relationship problems.

J.O. Can you tell me something about your experiences as a Head in Exeter?

M.S. I applied for the post because my father had been there at the end of the war and had spoken about some of the places with great affection, so I thought it would be rather nice to teach there, if it included promotion as well. I was ignorant of the fact that Devon has hundreds of applications. It was a funny sort of interview – a tour of the school in the morning, an interview in the afternoon with the Director of Education and some senior people, and then selection for a final interview in the evening.

The charm of that particular post was that it was a girls' secondary modern school, due to be amalgamated the following September with two mixed schools, one of which was Church of England, and a boys' school, to form a comprehensive. I thought it would be really good, really interesting to be involved in that, and indeed it was. Lots of people were appointed at the same time, and even though the school was going to be built around the former girls' school – a very nice site in Exeter – the existing staff felt vulnerable because they hadn't had to teach boys before and it was uncertain what was going to happen to all their jobs in the amalgamation. It was absolutely ideal for somebody like me who wanted to try out new ideas. I looked at things carefully, remembering that staff might be touchy, and prepared papers for consultation. I stressed that these were alternatives that we might consider, and asked for views. The pattern of not taking a step without consulting and getting the feel of things was ingrained by that time. It was very good indeed to actually reshape something, to introduce lots of new ideas. I had a staggered school lunch-time, for example, because we had limited dining facilities. I introduced a faculty system. I promoted a scheme whereby, for the summer term, all the children who were going to start in September came for one night a week and they had a youth-club programme of activities with our first-year children, and volunteer staff running it. So, I had plenty of opportunities. Some of the younger teachers were pleased to have something a bit different and a little livelier, and some of the older ones too were not uninterested.

J.O. Were you the only female secondary Head or were there others?

M.S. There was one other female secondary Head of a comprehensive school, and so we two were the only women.

J.O. Did you feel that the authority had considered the business of appointing in those terms?

M.S. I don't think so. My predecessor had been a woman, and of course the school was going to remain all-female for two terms, so I did feel, afterwards, that I might have had a slight edge at interview, because in the interim of two terms a woman might be useful. Then I decided, well no, not if they had any foresight, because what is two terms when you think about the lifetime that a Head might be in post?

J.O. And what about your time as Head here?

M.S. My predecessor had been the Head here when it was a secondary modern school, and he had been reappointed as Head when it became a comprehensive school in 1968, when it had about 480 on roll. But by the time I was appointed here, in January 1975, it was about 1,500. I thought the patterns that had been established were no longer appropriate to the school, so I set about using the experience I had in Exeter. For example, I thought a faculty system would be the way to restructure the academic side – there were about twenty different departments – but I had to consult, suggest models and try to get ideas to come from colleagues. Similarly, there was a house system which was wholly inappropriate to the school, because Gloucestershire had built house-rooms to accommodate groups of 120 pupils, and at that time we had 150 pupils in each group. We couldn't get them into the house-rooms – absolute bedlam it was, just trying to get the bodies in. I thought that a change to years, would be the sensible way of moving forward, but I didn't dictate to staff. I suggested to the Deputy Heads that we ought to rethink the pastoral-care groupings and asked how we should go about it. So we asked for volunteers who went to look at pastoral systems elsewhere and came back to report. Then we discussed all their findings and recommendations and then we made the decision.

J.O. What's the gender breakdown of your Deputy Heads – how many are women?

M.S. I've got three Deputy Heads – two men and one woman – a senior management quartet of two males and two females. We get on well together, both personally and professionally.

J.O. Were you always free to plan what you did, were you

always autonomous, or were there personal circumstances that you had to weigh up?

M.S. I stayed within travelling distance of home for quite some time, and then I took off, but my departure spoilt some personal relationships. I can think of a few that soured because I tended to put my professional commitments as a first priority. That was what I wanted to do, so it was very much a case of 'This is what I'm like: you must take me on my terms.' I don't have any regrets about it. I have never felt, 'oh dear, if only I had done this or done that,' because I have done what I wanted to do. I have been very lucky. I have had a very smooth career passage – very smooth indeed. It must be extremely difficult, I think, for women out of the profession even for a short space of time, to have children, to get back into the swim again. Especially in this last two or three years – a fortnight's sickness and you come back to find that the legislation has changed. Yes, I think to be successful, and confident in your role, friendly support is a prerequisite, but also a certain amount of ruthlessness, or selfishness, or single-mindedness is necessary if you set your sights on something and intend to go for it.

J.O. Do you get impatient with female colleagues who are less assertive, or do you encourage others?

M.S. I do encourage them, and it bothers me that some don't seize opportunities. I've anxieties about able women colleagues who won't try for posts because they're sensitive that their husbands' feelings might be hurt. I believe that they shouldn't put careers on back burners just to be supportive. That kind of thing makes me cross because, though it may ensure domestic harmony at the time, later it may cause professional frustration and resentment. There are some situations, of course, where you have to move to one side, or take a step back in order to be supportive, and that's perfectly valid, but when you are on an equal footing as professional people then it should be all-round equality.

CHAPTER 5

The Secondary Deputy

MOLLIE ROACH

Analysing my career for the purposes of this book, I am forced to realize that much of what has happened has been reactive and unplanned. In retrospect I realize that there has been, over the years, a gradual strengthening of purpose and resolve, but perhaps this too has been reactive, in that ambition – always a powerful motivator – has been strengthened and reinforced by increasing success and job satisfaction.

I learned to read early and was a bright child at school, seeking and gaining approval through academic success. I passed the eleven-plus and went to the local girls' high school. I emerged in 1958, with seven 'O' levels and two 'A' levels, having been for the most part the model of a well-motivated, anxious-to-succeed, anxious-to-please pupil. I went to UCW Aberystwyth to read English and History in 1958, but my university career was disrupted by marriage and child-bearing. I completed my second year in 1960, but it was not until 1973/4 that I obtained my degree, some fifteen years after I first started.

In 1967 my husband moved out of industry and attended the local teacher-training college to do a PGCE course. He began teaching in a local primary school later that year, the year that our second child started school. With a much easier domestic routine, and with a husband whose working hours were such as to make it possible for him to be more supportive in the home, I decided to apply to the same college for a place on the PGCE course. Although at that time I had not completed my degree, I was accepted for a one-year course, and the following year I joined the staff in the English department at a comprehensive school some thirteen miles away.

In fact, the school had just become a comprehensive, and I spent my first year travelling between the old grammar school, where the first year was based, and the new comprehensive on the hill, where the grammar and secondary modern pupils, and their staff, were settling into an uneasy and sometimes hostile relationship. The school was small and rural, and there were few women in any position of status or authority in the management structure. The Senior Mistress looked after the girls and filled the pastoral role. She did the job well and was a good teacher – firm but sympathetic. Most of the pupils respected her, and some liked her a great deal. I remember modelling my behaviour on hers – particularly in terms of classroom technique and manner – especially during the first couple of years, when survival and the retention of a reasonable amount of dignity were priorities!

The Head of English (who was also the Deputy Head) and the Headteacher – both male – were friendly, and supportive in the mode which is now recognized as paternal and patronizing. At the time, I did not think of it as such – simply feeling that they were kind, but largely distanced from me by their seniority and by the wide gulf in experience between us. Looking back, I feel that I may have done them an injustice, in that they were helpful, supportive and encouraging, but I feel now that it was all very informal and not very professional in its approach. It may simply be that the management style is different now – few of the outcomes have changed.

After having taken over responsibility for the library in the school, I followed a two-year part-time school-librarian course in Birmingham, travelling from Hereford to Birmingham every Saturday morning during term time. During the two years, I was 'promoted' to a Scale 2 in respect of my work in the library. I was also asked by the Headteacher to attend Lawrence Stenhouse's Humanities Curriculum Project course, at the University of East Anglia, and I became a founder member of the school HCP team. I became increasingly involved in the work of the school, helping to initiate a team-teaching approach in the English department, and co-writing and producing the Bromyard Play performed by the school in the local church.

Thinking about the possibility of promotion led me to the conclusion that worthwhile career progression was going to be difficult to achieve without a degree. The job market in the early

1970s was much freer than today, in that schools were larger and prospects generally were better, but without a degree it seemed that the best I could achieve would be second-in-department, and I had begun to realize that I was getting more out of working than 'just' the money.

My husband had just successfully completed a year's secondment following a B.Ed. course at Worcester Training College, and was contemplating a move into the secondary sector, where his earlier industrial experience might be of more value and where promotion might be more readily available. I applied to UCW Aberystwyth, and was told that it would be possible to take up where I left off and complete the degree course which I had left after two years in 1960. Herefordshire refused a secondment, but Shropshire – my original grant county – agreed that I was entitled to claim the final year of the mandatory grant. Both these career aspirations came to a head in 1973–4, when my husband got a job in the West Midlands and I decided to take up Aberystwyth's offer of a place. The children moved to Aberystwyth with me, and my husband commuted at the weekends.

On completion of my degree, I applied for and was offered a post in the West Midlands as Scale 2, second in the English department in a large urban comprehensive school. The set-up was 'traditional', in that most Heads of Department and most pastoral Heads were male, with the usual exceptions of the Head of First Year, the female Deputy, the Head of Girls' PE and the Head of Home Economics. The Head of English – a man – was actively seeking promotion, and within a year of my joining the school he left to take up a position of Deputy Head. I was made acting Head of Department, and when the post was advertised I successfully applied for it.

The school was very different from my previous school. It was more than twice as big and had all the problems of an urban school in an area of industrial decay, including a very high proportion of young, relatively inexperienced staff. The Headteacher was new to the school, and it seemed from comments passed by the 'old hands' that his management style was the opposite to that of the previous Headteacher, who had adopted a formal, traditional approach to the running of the school. For me, also, his approach provided a challenge, and one which I enjoyed. It was good to be able to put forward ideas without feeling hesitant about their reception, and to be in a position to encourage others to come forward with their own initiatives. I began to enjoy the staff-development aspect of the work of a Head of Department, and I got a great deal of satisfaction out of trying to create unity of purpose and a shared perception of the work of the department among the wide variety of individuals who taught English in the school – few of whom were English specialists, and many of whom were 'shared' with at least one other department.

This was at the time of the Bullock Report, and I began to work with colleagues across the curriculum in the development of a language policy for the school. I became a sixth-form tutor, and wrote and produced the staff Christmas-term play. The atmosphere of the day was such as to encourage development and change. I became aware of 'school management' as a concept and was encouraged to sign up for an educational management course at the local polytechnic. As I moved up in the hierarchy of the school, and from there 'out' into the inter-school world, I began fully to realize the advantageous position that I was in as a woman as regards my next career move. I was well-qualified in a major subject area of the curriculum; I had a proven successful record as a teacher in two widely differing schools, and in a variety of teaching situations; I had senior management experience of running a department; and, having to come into teaching late, I had what was perceived to be the 'necessary maturity'.

As I neared the end of my third year at the school, I saw advertized the traditional female Deputy job 'with responsibility for girls' discipline'. I had only recently begun to develop a positive relationship with the female Deputy at the school, and I sought her advice, hoping to be told that it 'wasn't too soon' to apply, and that I could 'use the opportunity to gain interview experience', if I was 'lucky enough' to be called. She obliged with precisely that advice, adding that it would be foolish to ignore such an opportunity.

I applied, was offered an interview, and got the job. The long list comprised ten to twelve people (one man). Only one other woman had a degree, and no one else had experience of running a large department. Several were from the 'girls' subject' areas of the curriculum and had little or no experience of teaching boys and of working 'with' as opposed to 'for' men. The short list included someone who was already a Deputy in a smaller urban school, seeking to widen her experience; the Head of Sixth Form from a nearby school; and a senior teacher with timetabling experience, whose previous experience was in a girls' school. I include this detail not out of a sense of false modesty, to explain my success, but to highlight the difficulties under which women labour, even when applying for 'women's' jobs, and to help define some of the attitudes and perceptions which are attached to the job of the female Deputy.

Before her appointment as Deputy Head, my predecessor had been Head of Needlework. I inherited responsibility for girls' welfare, the tuck shop and the stationery cupboard, and was pleased to take on responsibility for the pastoral aspects of the school's work. One of the other two Deputies, 'had' boys' discipline and examinations and the other 'had' administration and the timetable.

Over the years, we shared and exchanged opinions and ideas more and more, and the reality of team management began to develop in an informal, unstructured, organic response to the working situation. I extended my interests in staff development and training, and began to arrange and offer in-service training sessions to the staff and to be approached by staff seeking professional-development advice. When the TRIST initiative arrived, I became the school's TRIST coordinator, and was seconded by the LEA to coordinate the TRIST programme across the borough.

Before my secondment, I had conducted a series of staff-development interviews, helping staff to review their work so far, to consider their current situation and to set targets for the future, both short-term and long-term, as appropriate. On my return, I began the second phase of these interviews, involving the other Deputies as interviewers, and established a third phase in the following year, again getting considerable satisfaction and enjoyment from working with staff in a collaborative, cooperative situation. Through these interviews I began to develop a picture of the whole school, and an awareness of the perceptions of colleagues with regard to their situation *vis-à-vis* their peers, superordinates and subordinates.

I had always been an active member of the NUT at school level but during my time as Deputy Head I became involved at local committee level, and, as a member of JCP, in negotiations on local conditions of service with the LEA. I was President of the

WTA during the teacher action, and teacher representative on the education committee for a year.

Having reached a period of marking time as a Deputy with a well-defined role, which I was extending, and in a stable and sustained school situation, I found that the union offered the opportunity for a wider perspective, which I began to need to set against the inward-looking school-focused role of the Deputy. Moreover, the union's course for incoming Presidents focused on time management, control of meetings, negotiating skills and the like, and proved an excellent preparation for presidency. It also added considerably to my ability to perform these administrative and management tasks as a Deputy. On reflection, I am aware that I gained a great deal from my union involvement. Confidence in my ability to organize and control a meeting, to speak in public, to negotiate, to disagree and to register a dissenting minority viewpoint forcefully has been fostered and encouraged by my participation in union activities. I have also been aware of a considerable amount of support from female colleagues in the union – often when such support has been lacking elsewhere.

It must, I think, be significant that my involvement with the union developed at time when my professional life was perceived – possibly by myself, and probably by others – as being 'just the female Deputy', with my efforts to extend the role into INSET and staff development being seen as 'just finding herself something to do'.

I had been applying for headships for some time, and had been called to a couple of interviews, but with no success. I made several more applications – all in vain – and attempted to take stock as follows:

- It was no longer an advantage to be a woman, since governors seemed to prefer male Headteachers.
- All of the factors which had advantaged me so far, were now also advantaging the competition.
- The competition was stronger than in the 'women's job' situation, there was more of it, it was mostly male and it was mostly five to ten years younger than me, since child-rearing had delayed my entry into teaching by some eight years.

The TRIST secondment offered an alternative line of development, and, although in the immediate short term it did not result in a change of circumstance, headship applications began to be taken up again. I was called to interview, and felt much more positive about the whole procedure, even though I was not successful. In the longer term the experience gained in TRIST resulted in my present TVEI appointment. I am now in the first year of a two-year secondment to the LEA's TVEI programme, working in curriculum and staff development, and am aware again of a feeling of enjoyment in the wider, inter-school, whole-borough situation which I discovered while working in the TRIST project.

In attempting to identify 'lessons learned', turning-points and major influences in my career to date, I am aware that hindsight may lead to rationalization rather than to accurate analysis.

Why a teacher? Why English? The answer to both questions is gender-dominated. A teacher because, at the time I decided to train, I had two small children and the hours and holidays matched. English because I was good at it in school and had, therefore, studied it at university. I cannot recall the stage at which I realized/was told/decided that I was 'no good' at Maths or Science or Games, but it was quite evident early on that I was going to be, and therefore was, 'good at' the traditional girls' subjects – English, languages, the humanities and Biology. At the girl's high school which I attended, teaching and nursing were the accepted careers, and, if a pupil went to University, little was done to prepare her for the possibility of anything other than an academic career of some kind. Having started work as an English teacher in a small, rural secondary school, being a woman was helpful in that I was filling the expected role. I could do all the things I liked doing and which, by virtue of being a woman, I was assumed to be capable of doing – I could look after children, I could read a great deal, I could exhibit caring and sympathetic behaviour towards pupils and staff, and I could involve myself in creative, aesthetic, emotional activities such as drama and music. I could also tell people – especially the pupils – what to do, and I could perform administrative and clerical work in respect of my work in the classroom and in the school library.

Looking back, this a classically stereotyped 'career', but, at the time, I enjoyed it all very much. There is great satisfaction in doing what you can do, and doing it well. The difficulty comes when you have done it for so long that you don't feel competent to do anything else. When the Headteacher in my first school asked me to go on the HCP course, it was, perhaps, because of these gender factors, and I enjoyed the course and my subsequent work in the project because it called for an extension of the qualities which I have already outlined above as being gender-controlled/directed.

In deciding to return to university to complete my degree, I was recognizing that, although the pressure towards making teaching an all-graduate profession was only just beginning, it was clear that a teacher with a degree was more likely to get on than one without. I had at some point decided that I was not going to be just another 'pin-money' English teacher, and it is possible that my will to succeed came from another gender-related factor – the need to achieve recognition that challenged the stereotype of the role of women as being some way inferior. In conjunction with this, I could also identify a need for change, from one school to another or from one job to another; a willingness to accept, often uncritically, new opportunities and ideas; and a reaction against the gender stereotype of the female teacher settled in a familiar routine, accepting – often welcoming – a lesser role because 'it doesn't interfere with my domestic commitments.'

My career progression from English teacher to Head of Department was considerably eased by the gender factor. The subject, the teaching experience and the gender role reinforced each other. The Deputy Head post for which I applied was clearly gender-centred, in that it was 'tied' in the advertisement to 'a responsibility for girls' welfare and discipline'. It was the perception of the Headteacher, of the other two Deputies (both male) and of the governing body that the third Deputy 'should' be – 'ought' to be – a woman. The female Deputy post – tied, as it still is in the minds of the governing body, to responsibility for girls' discipline – is a mixed blessing in terms of women's career structure in education. If the concept did not exist, it is likely that many schools would have an all-male senior management team, and the 'minor' role of girls' discipline – perceived by all and sundry to be a mysterious and ill-defined 'legal necessity' – would be delegated to one of the women – Head of Girls' PE, Home Economics, Needlework or the like. On the other hand, the very existence of the post leads to an assumption that every school had three Deputies: one female, with a pastoral/girls' responsibility, and two male, in charge of the timetable, the curriculum, examinations, administration, boys' discipline etc. The majority of secondary Headteachers are male, and there are, therefore, very few schools where the senior management team is evenly split between men and women.

In my experience of application and interview for headships, the management ideal in teaching, as in most other professions, is contained in the concept of the male authority figure. Lists of criteria for selection of secondary-school Headteachers are likely to be gender-biased; questions and procedures employed during interview are such as to allow candidates to demonstrate these gender-biased qualities – in short, it seems as though a woman must demonstrate masculine attributes and qualities when in competition with men for such a post. That final phrase is important, since I have been involved in interview procedures for the headship of a girls' selective school which was perceived, like the 'female Deputy' to be 'a woman's job'. For this post, as for the female Deputy post, the 'normal' masculine management aspects of the work were secondary considerations in the interview procedures, which centred around behaviour and attitudinal concerns.

In addition to this 'masculine manager' syndrome, age became a gender factor, in that I went into teaching late, having spent eight to ten years in child-rearing. I was therefore 'behind' in the race, and increasingly found myself in competition with (mostly male) colleagues some eight to ten years younger than myself.

My first 'year out', to complete my degree, had a direct and beneficial effect on the job-satisfaction aspect of my career. The first secondment, to the LEA TRIST project, led back into school but altered my perspective. My current secondment, to the TVEI project, has a year still to run, and may lead to a similar post, either here or elsewhere. Increasingly in the last two years I have been contemplating the possibility of moving out of my present career line and into a job in TEFL, with VSO or the British Council or a similar organization. My husband is also considering a similar move. This also may be a gender-influenced inclination, in that I feel 'free' to do this now that my children are independent, though inhibited somewhat by an awareness of increasing pressures from ageing parents.

Considering my career in general, I feel that women Deputies could (and should) insist on acquiring experience in 'male' management areas, such as timetabling – not because this is a necessary prerequisite to headship but because it is generally perceived to be so, and a competence in this area would give more confidence at interviews. Women should avoid the temptation to do only what it is thought we are good at. This not only denies us several new experiences and competences; it also deprives male Deputy colleagues of the opportunity to develop the necessary skills and competences required for the traditional 'woman's role'. Additionally, it confirms both ourselves and others in the belief that competences and skills are gender-specific.

I find it difficult to assess my management style except in the most general of terms – participative and manipulative, which may well be gender-biased qualities. It is probably true that at first I found it difficult to establish a satisfactory professional working relationship with male senior management colleagues. Getting the working relationships on the 'right' basis took me a long time, and had as much to do with my own almost automatic response – based on a wish to fit into the picture which 'they' had of the way in which I should work – as it had on the reality of the situation, which was that at first I lacked the confidence, and the support, to be myself – especially if that meant a loss of approval or esteem (which seemed to me to be the same thing).

If I consider my experience, and try to draw on it to identify strategies for encouraging more women into management, it seems vitally important to provide more women role models. The lack of women in middle and senior management positions in schools inhibits others from trying. More women would be encouraged into middle and senior management if they had such examples before them already.

There are still too few women in those areas of the school curriculum which provide whole-school management experience across all the age and ability levels of the secondary school. At the subject/careers-choice stage, girls should be encouraged to think outside the obvious subject areas – career/life planning for women should include guidance which assists women to choose outside the stereotypes. On the other side of this coin, the traditional structures of the secondary school, reflecting the subject-based curriculum, could be made more flexible. This would allow women in minority subject-areas the opportunity to gain experience of management skills, and would, in addition, encourage a wider, less subject-oriented, perspective on the curriculum.

A more positive, more flexible, attitude towards training would also be helpful in giving women the confidence and experience necessary to encourage them to apply for and take up management positions. Evening, weekend and school-holiday in-service courses should have crèche and family facilities. Alternative forms of INSET – work shadowing, job share and similar strategies – would provide opportunities for women to develop and exercise management skills, and to become aware of, and confident in, their own potential.

The content, methodology and organization of management-training courses which do not recruit (and retain) at least as many women as men should be carefully reviewed, in order to address any imbalance.

The 'time-out-for-children' gap causes difficulties for women seeking promotion. More positive encouragement could be given by giving credit for years spent in childcare, as years in industry are credited, by making in-service training accessible to women during their absence while child-rearing, and by allowing part-time employment as part of a longer, paid, maternity-leave entitlement.

More women would be encouraged into middle and senior management if the philosophy and vocabulary of the whole concept of management were less gender-biased. Not surprisingly, current research into management styles results in lists of qualities, skills and behaviours which are in themselves 'masculine' in their orientation. Women should be aware that the whole study of management is dominated by the idea that management is for men. It would be both helpful and interesting to carry out 'neutral' research into the true nature of the skills and abilities required of managers at all levels and in all areas of work, including education – 'neutral' in the sense that the research is not influcenced by the predominantly male management situation which obtains in most areas of education, industry and commerce at present.

This account obviously reflects my experience, and is now probably somewhat out of date, even if the situation 'on the ground' shows, as yet, little evidence of change. Of the twenty secondary schools in the authority for which I work, only three have women Headteachers (and one of those is Head of the single-sex girls' school). Of a possible fifty-nine Deputy Heads, twenty-four are women. Yet, despite these figures, it is my impression that more women are coming forward for promotion to senior management-level posts, and that attitudes towards them are more positive. My impression is also that the younger generation of teachers – both male and female – is less likely to accept gender stereotypes and more willing to take a positive attitude towards equality of opportunity on gender issues. I would hope that this is reflected in the attitude of administrators and school governors when considering appointments, and that in turn these changes in attitude will be reflected in increasing numbers of women applying for, and being appointed to, positions in the management structure of education.

CHAPTER 6

The Primary Head

NANCY TRAQUAIR

I am the Head of a Birmingham primary school. I did not set out with the intention of becoming a career teacher, or even a teacher at all, but I don't think it is an accident that I ended up in education: women teachers were probably the only attainable career role models that working-class girls had. I went to university in Scotland and did an ordinary degree, and there is an implicit assumption that people with ordinary degrees will end up teaching. I trained at college and thought I would try teaching and then perhaps see what else I could do. My family didn't push me into teaching, but they certainly thought that it was a good job for a girl. I taught in Scotland in secondary schools: first Science for a couple of months, until my twins were born, then I worked part-time teaching Modern Studies and English. I then moved to Birmingham, because my husband wanted to do a postgraduate degree at the Centre for Contemporary Cultural Studies. He was still an undergraduate when we married and had the children. We had thought that he would get a grant and that I would be able to work part-time, but in the event he didn't get a grant and I decided to go for full-time work and he took on some of the responsibilities for the children.

I started teaching full-time in an inner-city multicultural primary school. I had no primary training or experience, and I had only ever worked in a white school. I'd also learned about teaching mainly as a part-timer, and that gave me a rather inadequate induction, especially as I had all the other pressing demands. I was very much left to get on with it, and it was a very difficult time. Eventually I learned to cope, but only by being very formal and keeping the children busy, rather than really helping them develop. I was very unhappy about this solution to control, but I didn't see a way of developing alternatives in that school at that time. I think that that period has made a difference to the way I work as a Head, as I understand the need for support and the isolation that new teachers can feel.

I learned a lot from an ESL teacher, saw ESL as a possible way of developing, and moved as a peripatetic teacher to two adjacent schools. I enjoyed being able to focus on specific areas – language development and the experience of black pupils – and felt I developed expertise. I became really engaged with the issues and, because all the peripatetic teachers came together one afternoon a week, I was able to work in groups with other teachers. I was also encouraged by senior teachers in the department to contribute to courses they organized for class teachers. However, after five years I did feel that I needed to move on, so I tried for two 'mainstream' jobs, without success.

I was lucky then in that there was a move to school-based in-service training in ESL, and joining the team that organized that changed my life. It was like going to university. There were five of us in the team, and we worked very well together. It was interesting, and we were breaking new ground. Until then I did see work as important to me – well, it was an economic necessity, and I have always felt that being a 'worker' was an important aspect of my identity – but it was not necessarily satisfying. There seemed too big a gap between what I got out of my job and what was important to me in my 'personal' life – the ideas or the politics. My husband had been a postgraduate student for most of the time I was an ESL teacher, and we had always had a notion that when he got a job it would be my turn – to develop, to do something interesting, more fulfilling – but joining the INSET team changed all that – I was so interested and excited by it. It also had a lasting impact on the way that I work, in that negotiating some of the relationships with teachers in the schools that we went to was difficult. I felt then that I always tried to avoid conflict – I wasn't ready to deal with that – but I think I learned the value of teamwork.

If I think about the subsequent development of my career, I have to say that I was lucky. I moved not because I didn't like what I was doing but because I started to think about the future. I was fortunate in that there was a promoted post in a school where the Head knew me and knew the work of the team. I think it would have been much harder to move to a mainstream job from INSET work if he had not had contact with the team and valued its work. I felt that I could work in that school and that I was in tune with the Head's values and the way he wanted to work. The job was advertised as a Senior Master/Mistress job, for language development, and I'd expected it to be a Scale 4. I felt very nervous about applying for what was in effect a Deputy's job. I didn't feel I had the authority or ability to take on a job of that nature rather than simply a specific curriculum responsibility, but I was encouraged by friends and colleagues, and I felt I had the language experience. I applied and I got it, but I am aware that my progress through promotion was very unconventional – I did not come through on the usual class-teacher route.

It was a clearly defined job, ideas in ESL were moving quickly, and I was anxious to put them into practice. I was there for four years, and I think there were changes in people's ideas about how to teach. Other things made a significant impact on the way I work. I became involved in training for women, I did assertiveness training and I began to think in a more self-conscious and developed way about a career – about what I really wanted to do. Looking back on that period, almost a decade ago, I remember it as a very positive time – a great time – when I felt I developed a lot and came to terms with some of the divisions between my personal and my work life. I would say it was one of the most fruitful periods for me, even though it coincided with two traumatic events – divorce and diabetes!

Once I started applying, I got a headship quite quickly. I was particularly attracted to the school – I just felt 'This is the one for me,' and perhaps that did it. I did know the authority very well, and I knew there were certain schools I would apply for.

My predecessor had been a woman, but there was a delicate situation in that the Head had been on secondment for two years and the male Deputy had been acting Head. We had to talk about this, and I had to deal with it. His approach to the job and to relationships was very different from mine, and I felt conflict was more likely to arise with him. I tried to deal with this by defusing the situation, because I wanted to support him as Deputy but I didn't feel the aggro was necessary. This is such a commonplace characteristic of men in authority, and I have noticed a difference in women's treatment of such difficulties.

If I try to generalize from that particular example to ways of describing my management style in relation to gender differences, then I suppose I would stress the informality. I know perfectly well that there's a difference between formal procedures and what actually happens, so I know formal procedures aren't enough. Nobody stands on their dignity in the school. I think I'm good at generating enthusiasm and stimulating activity. A woman Deputy has been appointed now, and she's made a considerable difference. The relationship between us is more open and less 'managed'. We have a similar outlook and style. I feel very supported by her and the work she does.

It is difficult to set out a clear agenda for 'female' headship. I'm still not particularly comfortable with some conventional aspects of being a Head. I don't like to refer to 'my' school or 'my' staff. I deliberately don't have a key to the school, which surprises some people who feel that I should be able to get in at any time I like, but I don't think of the school as mine.

I have put a clear and explicit structure in place, and I see my job as having a clear vision for the school and trying to build consensus around that – but not by telling people what to do. It isn't possible to be completely democratic and to get away entirely from hierarchy, but it is possible to make people feel involved in decisions and that they have a stake in decisions. Working like this is very time-consuming, and it is still necessary to take the initiative and to meet people's expectations of leadership while encouraging them to feel entitled to modify proposals or to contribute to them. As well as having clarity about structure and process, there needs to be an ethos or a culture which encourages participation. That participation can't be equal, because, as Head, you are bound to have access to more information, you'll have spent more time thinking about a problem and you'll be clearer about what you want to do. I think women in senior positions – myself included – feel some discomfort about the hierarchical and inequitable aspects of management, but they are inevitable. What I'm attempting is acceptance of the responsibility I have for the ethos and direction of the school, but as a community which is self-consciously engaged with its management. Otherwise schools are victims of the sort of upheaval I saw when I took over – if they're very dependent on a particular Head and style of headship, how do they carry on if that Head goes? I do need to provide direction – that's a responsibility and a duty, and people have a right to it – but it must be done in collaboration and through teamwork. It's much more fundamental than coming to the school and saying 'I want to get to this.' It's more to do with taking the whole school with you and working for fundamental change.

These are complex issues, about which I've reflected at length, and there are no easy routes to becoming an effective manager. I think that women, for whatever reasons, tend to attempt to work with people and try to take them with them rather than set up conflicts and allow divisions. But there's also the need that women have to allow people to participate and their reluctance to close down options and 'take a lead'. Leadership is such a difficult concept. Perhaps its a bit like motherhood – you want to encourage independence. I've certainly worried that staff think I'm too tentative. I think I may be too tentative, because personal relations are important: I want a happy school because I think that that is productive and motivating, and perhaps I've not stated certain things clearly enough.

Trying to achieving this is challenging, and time-consuming, and these days it's often a question of crisis management. But it is still worth the effort for a more planned, developmental and supportive approach.

CHAPTER 7

The Head of Department in Teacher Education

JOAN WHITEHEAD

The invitation to write this chapter produced two responses from me which are probably revealing (and possibly shared by other contributors and readers). First, would those who had been significant in shaping my beliefs and actions be flattered or offended if they read it, and, second, would my contribution be judged as self-indulgent and not 'real' academic work?

The first reaction reveals the strength of early socialization. I am the only daughter and the youngest child of a northern church-going family, and I attended a strict, single-sex academic grammar school where consideration of others was the primary virtue. I was drilled to please family, god or teacher, and it has taken many years for me to be more my own person. I knew that to write authentically could risk giving offence.

My other concern – that such writing wouldn't be seen as proper academic work – reveals the dominance of masculine definitions of research as 'objective', technical, scientific and impersonal. Although intellectually I supported how these definitions have been substantially challenged by qualitative methodologies, including feminist writing and life-history work, I had not tested my own intellectual commitment by engaging in such writing myself. Contributing to this chapter has provided me with that opportunity and has helped me identify with other women engaged in the difficult process of defining and redefining management in education.

I am Head of a very large department of initial teacher education, with over 1,000 students. The department is not only large, it is extremely complex, as it offers a variety of primary and secondary training routes. Furthermore, the design of these courses –

particularly the four-year B.Ed. – adds a further layer of complexity. I came to the polytechnic from a background in teacher education, with some experience of managing courses, though not on the scale that I have had to undertake in my two years here. Writing this chapter has caused me to reflect on those years, and to assess them from the perspective of the woman manager in HE. It has prompted me to reflect upon the sources on which I have drawn to do the job – particularly those elements of my previous experience and those aspects of my educational and social philosophy which have shaped my relationships with colleagues. It has also led me to an examination of the difficulties I faced as a woman in becoming a Head of Department, and which I continue to face. I do not intend this chapter to be read as a set of notes on 'how to do it'; rather, it is an attempt to share with others facing similar situations the lessons learned from my particular voyage into the relatively uncharted territory of being a woman manager.

There are very few useful academic texts on women in management. I did not have a management background, in any case, so I relied on feminist and sociological literature which I had studied and taught, and on what I suppose are best described as general principles about the treatment of others, some of which I had learned from the experience of working in particular groups, and some of which I had learned from being managed.

My career began in 1967, when I qualified at the London Institute of Education and took up an Assistant Lecturer post at Loughton College of Further Education. I had visited the college as a student and felt in tune with the educational philosophy of the General Studies department and with the management style of the Head. He and several women staff were socialists, and it was a young, vibrant community in which as a newly qualified teacher I felt I would be enabled to develop further as well as to make a positive contribution. I felt a sense of shared values, a common identification of purpose. My time at Loughton was among the most informative and enjoyable of my career. This isn't simply nostalgia for youth and the heady days of the 1960s, when resources were abundant, teacher-led innovation and developments were welcomed, teacher professionalism was respected and I was still free from childcare responsibilities: the management style and ethos of Loughton provided me with a resource on which I continue to draw.

Rapid promotion from Assistant to Lecturer I and II was a

reflection of the time. The college was new and I was additionally fortunate in having a Head of Department who in principle and practice was an enabling manager, able to recognize the potential in relatively inexperienced staff, to promote and support their development and growth, and to provide opportunities which could, and in my case did, lead to career diversification. A characteristic of his management style, premised largely on his political affiliations and one I share and have attempted to emulate, was his overt expression of trust and confidence in the potential of others – staff and students – as well as his commitment to a more socially just and democratic society. Considerable loyalty was generated through such practice, and staff came to see their abilities recognized, valued and used. The department became well-known for its committed staff, its innovative teaching, its course development and the quality of its work with students.

The untimely death of Loughton's HOD coincided with an approach for me to take up a part-time post in teacher education at Goldsmiths' College. I had worked in teacher education as Associate Tutor at the London Institute, but I had not seriously contemplated a career switch. Despite being promoted within Loughton, I had never really planned a future career. I was established in further education, and moving from a full-time to a part-time contract made no financial sense. Indeed, in career terms it was risky, and the Goldsmiths' post offered limited opportunity to use the administrative skills I had developed. Nevertheless, supported by my partner, I decided to take the risk.

The transition into higher education was at times intellectually exhilarating, at other times isolating and difficult. In my first appointment the familiar culture of the department had been of great significance; the culture of the department I was to join at Goldsmiths' was unknown. As a newcomer to higher education, I rather naïvely expected some induction. There was none! I found myself in a department of conflicting interests around different sociological perspectives with no clearly articulated direction or mission. I was the only teacher educator in a male-dominated department, and it was an uphill struggle. However, I was soon appointed full-time and had considerable freedom and autonomy to develop work with students, to read and reflect, and to register for a master's degree, during which I was to form close, supportive relationships.

There was a considerable contrast in management style from

my previous institution. In higher education, management appeared to be viewed as a less worthwhile activity by a number of staff intent on exploiting to the full their individual academic reputations but without any corporate identity. This seemed to accord with Handy's description of an organization with a person culture, typical of universities, and geared primarily to the talents of individuals. The reality in this case, however, was management without any clear direction or purpose. I subsequently learned that the staff attitudes I observed there were not necessarily typical of higher education, nor of management practice in higher education, but they added to my stock of knowledge about managerial practices and staff responses to them.

The double burden or dual career – a bit of both?

By this time I was almost thirty; I had been married for seven years, and my partner and I both wanted children. The fact that I had met so few women academics in higher education confirmed my suspicion that one of the most difficult problems for women who wish to continue to develop academically and to continue to engage in activities which allow them to demonstrate their competence and so get onto the career 'ladder' is the difficulty of maintaining such activity at the same time as having young children. It may no longer be the case that the 'choice' facing women is not to have a family at all, but the 'career break' remains the single most important factor in depressing women teachers' promotion prospects (Evetts 1987). I also experienced at this time that other major difficulty in women's development of a conventional 'career path' – my partner had taken up a post in the South-West.

For a while we coped with this. We sold the house, lived separately and commuted at weekends, and we put off having children. During that year, a job was advertised at a college of education in the city where my partner worked. I recognized that my domestic arrangements would become easier and my desire for a family more realizable were I to be appointed. I also, however, felt that my career prospects were being threatened. It was not that I had a clear career route mapped out which the job change would interrupt – few women do, since most recognize the likelihood of disruption. It was was more that I had to face the prospect of giving up a work environment I had come to value, and where there was a considerable amount of stimulus and support.

Convincing the interview panel that I had a sound motive for applying for a job similar to the one I already held but in a smaller college presented an interesting problem. Employers then (although arguably less so now) tended to define the male career as the significant one in a dual-career household. If I gave my partner's location as my reason for wanting the job, I would be reinforcing that stereotype, and also devaluing my own commitment to the post and my capacity to do it, especially in competition with men who made reference only to 'professional' motives in support of their candidature.

Nevertheless, I was appointed. The world I was to enter and remain in for the next fifteen years presented a stark contrast to the cosmopolitan environment and the inner-city schools I had left. Although I acknowledged my good fortune in finding another job with comparative ease, I initially resented the move and frequently returned to London at weekends.

I began my new post with the intention of completing my master's degree at the London Institute, but at the same time I was constructing courses from scratch, and I also had my first child. That in particular was problematic, as the college wasn't used to married women staff, and my wishing to continue to work while pregnant gave considerable anxiety. I was warned by a Principal who subscribed to the notion of maternal deprivation that I would 'breed delinquents'. My Head of Department was very paternalistic, but supportive. I took the statutory maternity leave, but had to sacrifice my master's degree. The experience of 'choice' between career/academic development and family is a common one for women, and it is very difficult not to regret the lost opportunity for academic development.

The early years in my new post were characterized by frequent bouts of guilt and feelings of inadequacy. There was the assumption that it was somehow possible to achieve successful work performance, successful academic career, successful marriage and successful motherhood, and yet the reality was that each from time to time was tested. Each was demanding. Moreover, there was no attempt on the part of the college to make life any easier in terms of childcare facilities or flexible working or assistance with extended study.

Despite the pressures, I recognized that, unlike the majority of older female staff at the college, my generation had been offered the 'choice' of combining work with family responsibilities, and I knew that my life was envied by some. My choice was something to enjoy, despite its obvious physical and emotional demands. I also acknowledged the privileged position I was in as a professional woman in a dual-career household with sufficient money to pay for good childcare and domestic help.

The combination of raising a young family and work did, however, lead me to accept the impossibility at that time of progressing my career through promoted posts with large administrative responsibilities. I continued to be committed to work, but in a career sense I knew I was 'marking time'. Increasingly I came to regret not having completed my master's degree, and by the time my second child was a toddler I had decided to register as a part-time student at Bristol University while continuing to teach and to raise the children.

By this time I had a new woman Head, promoted from within the department, and I was granted a sabbatical term to work on my dissertation. The combination of a new female Head of Department, who was and remains a close friend and whose values were coincident with my own, and the intellectual confidence gained from completing the master's degree and publishing an article recharged me.

When the college decided to develop its own M.Ed. course, I was encouraged to apply and became the Course Leader. The experience of welding together a team of very disparate staff, helping them to use their talents, to develop a common philosophy and to work under pressure, to meet deadlines and ensure quality, was significant in my management development. It allowed the skills I had acquired in the early years of my career to surface. At this time I also became involved in a number of key committees in the college and worked closely with a new woman Assistant Director. She provided a model of organizational efficiency, with high standards of professionalism together with public appreciation for work accomplished. I became involved in various LEA initiatives and learned to listen to and work alongside individuals with very different political and educational commitments from my own – a valuable grounding for subsequent committee work.

I began, however, to feel rather trapped. My Head of Department left and I found considerable contradictions in the theory and practice of the new male incumbent. The fact that my own course management was successful but taken for granted and there were no promotion prospects led me to seek for research opportunities with management support. This was unforthcoming, and some painful encounters ensued. Through these I learned a considerable amount about handling stress, about the negative effects of inflexible management practice, and about the pressures that can drive individuals to act in particular ways. These experiences are ones on which I have continued to reflect as a senior manager.

It was then that my current post at the polytechnic became vacant. To move to a much larger institution and into a significantly larger management post was a quantum leap. The decision to apply took a long time to reach and was prompted as much by an increasing sense of alienation from the post I held as by the attraction of a new, different and more challenging environment – classic push and pull factors. It was again certainly not a 'planned' career move. During the interview for this post, and constantly since, I have had to confront and reappraise my management style. At the interview I felt on a knife-edge. I understood the need to convince the panel of my capacity to manage in the way in which management was conventionally understood – good organization and planning, clear aims, support for the department's policies, and ability to fit into the existing male executive group with a strong and well-respected Dean. I also felt the need to emphasize those capacities which I believed to be important: enabling, facilitative attributes which are generally seen as more 'female'. I had to make my own management principles clear in order that, should I be appointed, these were known, respected, able to be integrated into the prevalent culture and given a chance to flourish. Prior knowledge of the department also convinced me that such principles were worth stressing, since I saw among the staff a tremendous source of talent, expertise and creative energy. I saw my job as a manager being to value, draw on and use this resource and channel it in ways which would improve the teacher-education courses as well as bring personal and professional reward and satisfaction to staff.

The offer of the post brought a similar thrill of excitement as had my first appointment. I felt a sense of privilege in joining a department whose policies and endeavours I supported, but I also felt apprehensive about the scale and scope of the job.

In fact it was not at all easy. I felt an initial scepticism from several men as well as heightened expectations from some women – expectations that I would be more approachable and be able to deliver on as well as champion equal-opportunities issues. I could not tell whether the scepticism came from the same dismissive attitude to management that I had experienced earlier at Goldsmiths'. Whatever the cause, scepticism was short-lived. Determined to survive the pressures – for I am fundamentally a tenacious person – I set myself some priorities. I did so in order both to establish my competence within the department and with external bodies and to live out the enabling style of management to which I am committed, particularly with those for whom I had a direct line-management responsibility. Helping staff gain success in course validations and accreditations gave us all a sense of achievement. These activities provided scope for team-building, and for establishing my expectations about quality and standards. What I was unable to do sufficiently was to delegate. It is difficult to find the balance between enabling others and releasing control – or rather, if I put it more honestly, losing control. I suspect that my difficulty stems in part from fear of harsh judgement of performance by others, and this may be a characteristic of women managers.

At the practical level the job change was smooth: my domestic arrangements remained intact, and the polytechnic was within commuting distance. I had the continued support of friends, which relieved some of the isolation that I had anticipated.

I had expected that once in a senior management position I would feel isolated both from other women and in the male management team. I recognized that risk, and the strategies I adopted for reducing it included accessibility. I was much more accessible and publicly appreciative of colleagues than other members of the executive. However, a distance existed in terms of relaxation and general sociability. This was partly a result of the volume and pace of work, but it was also a matter of choice: it was a considered part of my management principles. This may seem contradictory in someone committed to working with and through others, but I believed it to be a necessary protection both for myself and for colleagues, particularly on those occasions where management responsibility is to call staff to account. I continue to reflect on this aspect of my practice, especially since the arrival of a woman Executive Head and Dean, who has a commitment to collegiate management within and beyond the executive, and where the potential conflict of friendship and role also exists.

There is no doubt that becoming a woman Head in a large department – even one with a clearly articulated equal-opportunities policy – has been challenging. I am still learning, and my commitments to developing staff include my own continued development. I am aware that this account may emphasize the problems at the expense of the satisfaction and pleasures, but it would be foolish to conceal the former as they do abound, particularly for women choosing to combine motherhood with a career. However, the skills one develops in order to balance, reconcile and manage conflicting demands are some of the skills on which senior managers daily draw. These are listening skills, planning and organizational skills, the holding together of a multiplicity of agendas, managing time, and moving from the relatively trivial and inconsequential to the significant. It is important to see the complementarity rather than the conflict – the sites are different, the scale is different, but there is much that is common. Men could do well to recognize this, for their own lives and careers as well as for those of their partners.

Looking back on my career, the lessons I learned observing others manage were undoubtedly significant in helping inform my particular practice, as was the background understanding of management I gained from organizational and educational studies, industrial sociology and women's studies. All these lessons have come to shape my own personal, professional and political commitments. Undoubtedly I prioritize good organization through the management of people – it is management to enable rather than to disable and control. I hope it's usually experienced in that way.

Reference

Evetts, J. (1987) 'Becoming career ambitious: the career strategies of married women who became primary headteachers in the 1960s and 1970s' *Education Review*, 39, 1.

CHAPTER 8

From HMI to Polytechnic Director

PAULINE PERRY

Writing about one's career is a challenge at once exciting and painful. Exciting because to be asked to reflect upon one's personal feelings and experience gives them an importance and a validity which for me, and I would guess for the majority of women, is an unusual experience. The habit of self-denial and self-denigration runs so deep that to talk about one's experience as if it might have value and worth carries with it the guilty and surprised pleasure of forbidden fruit. Painful too, because reflecting back over one's career brings back old embarrassments about the patchy and ragged nature of a career which included the birth and rearing of four children, and the inevitable break in full-time work which this caused. I have taught myself no longer to sound apologetic about the all-too-familiar career pattern of the career mother, but I have not yet quite taught myself to overcome the feelings of awkwardness, experienced over the years, in trying to explain to male interviewers and male bosses why my career did not follow the smooth upward pattern which they themselves had enjoyed.

My generation of women must have experienced more changes in their role, and in the expectations of society towards them, than any single preceding generation. Born in the years of the great depression in the Thirties, we became adults in the Fifties, and enthusiastically joined in the feminist revolution of the swinging Sixties. As Barbara Raskin says of our generation, in her brilliant book *Hot Flashes* (1988:23):

> Back in the Fifties, because we couldn't think of anything else to do, we carefully selected our china, glassware and silver patterns,

registered at the nearest department stores, and got married so
that we could proceed with our lives . . . While many of our
husbands became famous, most of us didn't . . . Few of us accomplished half of what we were capable of doing. We squandered
our expensive educations, mishandled our careers, and toyed
recklessly with our talents. We took our husbands' work seriously
and our own lightly.

So we did; and yet we are the generation that established a gender
revolution which will be hard to reverse in future decades, and
many of us, though we have moved from the feminism of the
1960s and 1970s into the more moderate post-feminist era, nevertheless owe much to that incredible experience of energy and
power which came from the early flowering of feminism.

To understand where one is now, it helps to look back to how
one arrived at the present. Much of what I believe about my role
today as polytechnic Director stems from the experences of my
immediate and distant past, and, although I am anxious to
explore the lessons of the present, I will start by acknowledging
my debts to the past.

I cannot begin without acknowledging what I owe to the
women of my own family. In my mind, I begin with my great-
grandmother. The mother of my mother's mother was married in
the mid-nineteenth century to a ship's captain in Sunderland. By
him she had seven children, the oldest girl of whom was my
grandmother. When the ship's captain was killed at sea, she was
left near destitute. There were no pensions nor provision beyond
charity for widows and small children, and, from being a relatively comfortable member of a leisured class, my great-
grandmother found herself obliged to take in other people's
washing in order to keep her children fed. The four oldest boys
went out to work to contribute to the family's expenses, and my
grandmother, then aged ten, helped her mother with the endless
loads of washing. When we were children, she would tell my
sister and me about her early-morning job rolling the big barrels
full of washing and soapy water across the yard of her home
where her mother would pound them with the wooden dolly until
they were clean, when she again would roll them down the yard
to drain away the water.

This story so far is no different from that of many thousands of
other children of my grandmother's generation. What makes this
story unusual is that her mother – my great-grandmother – was

so determined that her daughter should rise above her present circumstance that, despite her poverty, she paid out the penny a week needed for my grandmother to finish her studies at dame-school. In telling this story my grandmother would boast that she was the quickest and cleverest girl in the class, because she was so determined to save her mother's money that she completed all her studies by the age of eleven, instead of the normal twelve, in order to leave school and work at home a year early.

When my grandmother in her turn married, and became the mother of two daughters, she vowed that they would go to college: this was in the days before the First World War days when very few women were educated beyond the age of fourteen. My mother told me of the nightly battles which her parents would fight over the question, her father insisting that girls got married anyway and it was a waste of time and money to send them to college. My grandmother stood firm, however, and my mother trained both as a teacher and as a musician, gaining her teacher's certificate and becoming an Associate of the London College of Music.

Neither my grandmother nor my great-grandmother was a woman of means, nor was either of them the recipient of an extensive form of education. What each in her own way had was a confidence in their daughters, a determination to give them something which was their own personal possession of enlightenment and knowledge and, above all, which gave them a sense of identity beyond being somebody's wife and mother. This price-less gift was passed on to me from at least three generations of women by my mother, and I believe it to be an essential ingredient in my own sense of identity.

When I graduated, in the 1950s, marriage was a career. I married six weeks after receiving my degree in the Senate House in Cambridge, and in the next fourteen years (the majority of which were spent in North America) I worked full-time for just over four years. For eleven years I worked in part-time jobs, wrote books and articles, even involved myself in writing for radio and television, but all of this on a part-time basis. My 'career' was to make a home for my husband and four children, and not until my youngest son reached nursery-school age did I begin anything which could be described as a career of my own.

Those years are, however, an important part of the story. They demonstrate, I hope, that women do not have to choose between family or a career, as most of our mothers had to choose. Men have always expected to pursue their careers as well as enjoy family life, and any claim for justice or equality must expect the same for women. Perhaps where the feminist movement went wrong in the early 1960s was to suppose that we could forget all that part of ourselves which yearned for motherhood, and could try in every way to be single-minded career women with no concern for home and family. I am pleased that the women's movement has now turned away from that stance. It imposed an almost unbearable burden on each individual woman, since all attention had to be directed towards individual solutions to the conflict between job and home, instead of being directed towards the creation of structures in society which recognized that all human beings, male or female, have family concerns and commitments as well as loyalty to and enthusiasm for their work outside the home. I would like to see society at every level – government, employers, the public service and the community in which families live – recognize that small children, with all their needs for parental support and company, are a real part of all aspects of our lives – as real as any company or organization. When society can find a way to adjust both to the needs of the family and to the needs of the employment economy, without expecting women to bear the total sacrifice of either demand, the better and more whole will all our lives be.

For me, those years at home with my young family were, in the true sense of the word, fallow years, providing nourishment for the years ahead. In them I learned a great deal and acquired many skills which it would have been hard to acquire through any other experience, and which stand me in good stead as a manager today. A very dear elderly neighbour once described motherhood's tasks to me as 'teaching our children how to do without us'. She was right, of course, and to teach our children to grow up and be independent is the most important task we have as parents. To do it well, we must have trust and patience: trust that they can do for themselves as well or better than we could do for them; patience to wait while they make their mistakes on the way to independence. I frequently find myself today drawing on that experience if I feel a reluctance to allow someone to do a job which is of vital importance to the organization and where my erroneous instincts would lead me to keep too close a hand upon it. Trust in the individual and patience with the occasional mistake pay rich dividends.

Children also teach us to listen. Small children have none of the inhibitions of polite society and will make their wants and feelings known with a bluntness which we ignore at our peril. We quickly learn that the family is more harmonious, and tasks are performed more effectively, if people's feelings are taken into account, and if they feel they have real control of what they are doing. A style of management, like a style of parenthood, which simply says 'because I tell you so' is not effective for long.

So I do not deride the years anyone may have spent in raising young children. They are not barren but rich, and intelligently used, placed in context, and given the status they deserve as an integral part of society's survival they should be seen as an important part of the career development of any man or woman who is lucky enough to have spent periods of their life cycle walking at a child's pace through the world.

The social psychologist Eric Berne believed that there are three essential characteristics of the mature personality: spontaneity, awareness (as a child is aware of birdsong), and a capacity for intimacy. Surely these are indeed the characteristics well learned from time spent with children.

The feminist movement of the early 1960s in the United States was a heady experience. Although now we may revise some of the extreme positions of those early days, I believe there are some lessons which have been learned, and I hope learned forever. Above all, those of us who experienced those days in the USA learned the strength of women working together in networks of mutual support. I have derived enormous strength over the years from the instant recognition that women working as a minority in a man's world have for each other – the warm, reassuring 'Hail, sister' experience as we meet each other, perhaps in international gatherings, in social encounters or across the table of a committee room. I feel total distaste for any woman who carries into professional encounters the same competitive seeking for the attention of men which used to characterize the generation before us, for whom men were the only route to power. The women of the Western world have accomplished so much by learning to work together in the past twenty-five years, and it is exciting now to devote the energy derived from our own experience to help those women in the developing world whose fight for full membership of the human race is still in its beginnings. I commend the British Council for setting up a task force on women in the developing countries, and I am pleased and privileged to be one of its members.

Education was, for me, an inevitable choice of career when I became free to choose. It is, above every other institution in society, the vehicle through which women can achieve a measure of the psychological and economic independence which they need in order to be equal partners in both home and market-place. I spent three of the most exciting years of my career, before I joined HM Inspectorate, in charge of an access course for mature women who were to enter teacher training within the Oxford University Area Training Organization. Almost 100 women passed through the course during those three years, and it was a real reward indeed to see the anxious housewives who began the course with low self-esteem and no sense of their own intellectual strength turn into confident students, achieving beyond their wildest dreams. They were always ruthlessly self-critical, and yet they began gradually to understand the reasons for their previous low achievement, as they read Betty Freidan and other feminist writers and shared with each other the insights their experience was giving them. The friendships and the fun which were part of those years were an unlooked-for and won-derful bonus. An even greater bonus is to meet many now who have become Heads of schools, advisers or other senior members of the profession.

Involvement in the women's movement also gave me, like so many other women of my generation, an understanding of the source of that inchoate and unfocused anger which we had inher-ited from our mothers and their mothers before them. The anger sprang from so many roots: from wasted talent, from being a non-person, from the daily humiliation of helping others to live successful lives with no opportunity to engage in them ourselves. All this, which we had never understood but frequently felt, was brought out, examined, understood, focused and therefore dis-missed. Being free of that debilitating and crippling anger allowed all one's energy and life-force to become a controlled and enjoyed power source. Paradoxically, perhaps, it also made it easier to love one's children in a way which set them free – neither asking dependence from them nor burdening them with one's own.

In 1970 I became a member of Her Majesty's Inspectorate, in

the Department of Education and Science. It was not until after I had taken up my post that I was told that the Senior Chief Inspector had promised the HMI Association that the number of married women in the Inspectorate would never be 'more than the fingers of one hand'. There were, in fact, four of us appointed at the same time, and very firm friends we were and are to this day. The overwhelming majority of HMI were the best colleagues I had ever had or could hope to have, and neither showed nor felt one whisper of prejudice. Nevertheless, HM Inspectorate – known for many decades as 'the Brotherhood' – gave me my first experience of one or two members of that tiny minority of educated men who felt it appropriate to express their prejudice against working mothers quite openly. In my first few weeks in the Inspectorate I had the very painful experience of being told at the point of introduction to one older colleague, 'I think you should know that I did not support the introduction of married women into the Inspectorate, and I am totally opposed to latch-key children!'

I felt a deep personal satisfaction when the first woman Senior Chief Inspector was appointed as Head of HM Inspectorate. Sheila Browne was an exacting mistress, whose praise and approval was well worth working and waiting for. It was she who called me to her office to tell me that I was to be promoted to Staff Inspector from January 1975, thus creating the precedent of a married woman Staff Inspector (others were soon to follow). I also was then, and remained for the next five years, the youngest Staff Inspector in HM Inspectorate. I might perhaps be forgiven the thought which flashed instantly through my mind when I was told of the promotion. I recalled vividly one of the more painful experiences of my first few months in the Inspectorate, when I was working with an older male colleague who had bored me intensely with his calculations of his own promotion chances. Hoping to end his monologue, I had cheerfully remarked that it was more important, in my view, to enjoy the job than to worry too much about promotion. At this he broke into loud cackles of laughter, and replied, 'Well, of course, there's no question of your thinking about promotion! No one would be such a damn fool as to promote a married woman with four kids!'

In 1981 I was promoted Chief Inspector (the first time there had been 'Mrs' after the title 'CI' too), and for almost five years I was also the only woman in the DES senior management team.

Although the civil-service statistics show that it is still not easy for women to reach the higher ranks, nevertheless I think there would be few women in the senior ranks of the civil service who would claim any prejudice or handicap. By its tradition, the civil service rewards those who deliver, who communicate well and who work collaboratively rather than competitively with their colleagues. The generation of women now in their late thirties and early forties, available for promotion into the top ranks of the service, is of very high calibre indeed. Already the number of women at Under-Secretary and Deputy Secretary rank is growing, and in the next decade there should be a much healthier balance between the sexes, which must augur well for the service itself. It will be much easier not to be the only woman, not to have the wrong pitch of voice in discussions, not to be the only patch of colour at a table surrounded by dark suits.

Being a woman HMI, then Staff Inspector and Chief Inspector, probably parallels in many ways the experience of any woman moving through senior posts in the education service. One learns fairly quickly to identify those men who have real problems in working with, or even communicating with, women. There are men who visibly relax with relief when they can turn to a man in discussion rather than making what to them is the supreme effort of trying to communicate with a woman. There are men who cannot look at a woman as they talk, and men who play childish games of superiority by 'talking down' to a woman colleague or even boss. There were bizarre experiences in visiting colleges or schools, of course. I remember once deliberately outsitting a college Principal who sat and waited for me to pour the coffee which his secretary had brought in to the room! Others would suggest (to their cost, I fear!) that I might like to confine my inspection visits to Home Economics and Hairdressing. For most of these experiences I can genuinely say I felt only pity for the men whose lives were so narrow that they excluded one-half of the human race from their working relationships. It is small wonder, though, that sometimes women exhibit the characteristics that men are so quick to admire in each other, and so quick to condemn in our sex – by which I mean those characteristics of assertiveness, of insistence on being heard, even of shouting other people down when one's opinions are not being listened to!

My first Chief Inspector spoke to me most wisely when I started work for him as a newly promoted Staff Inspector. He told me that I would find two kinds of reactions from my former colleagues: 'Those who were your friends but who now no longer wish to be so; those who were not your friends before but who will now suddenly seek to become so. It is a judge of your character which you find the more painful.' He was very right. It was indeed painful – and I think it is still more painful for a woman than for a man – to find that one is no longer 'one of the gang' but in a senior position. Colleagues who were friends now appear in a different light when one is responsible for meeting deadlines to which their work must contribute or arranging team-work where their cooperation is needed. The lazy and slipshod will try to plead former friendship to get by with inadequate work, and the first test of management comes when such pleas must be resisted if the job is to be done satisfactorily. I do believe women find this very hard. Our rearing from childhood has been towards compliance, our motivation to please and to make friends. I found many men (and even some women) who would use my perceived female vulnerability to try to win sympathy for their own inadequacy: 'You will understand, Pauline, I am having problems with my health' or '. . . at home.' Over the years, I have discussed this kind of experience with many other women in management positions, and all have agreed that during the first year at least after becoming a manager this was one of the most difficult things with which they had to come to terms.

The other kind of reaction – that of those who never found time for a junior colleague or equal before, but now suddenly sought to be noticed, and to draw attention to their virtues – presented one of the more surprising and sad aspects of human nature. It was my first real experience of the vulnerability and insecurity of men. Having had no brothers, I had learned only from watching my sons grow up about the insecurities and anxieties of the male sex. It came as a surprise to me, however, to realize that middle-aged men, who seemed very confident when I had been their equal, felt a tremendous need for recognition and reassurance from one who was senior to them. Seeing oneself through the eyes of subordinates is an essential characteristic for any manager, and one of the lessons many women have to learn as they move into management posts is that they are perceived to have power and influence over others, which may seem threatening to their subordinates. It is not a concept which comes easily to most women: the temptation to say 'But its only me – nobody could possibly find me intimidating' is very strong.

But recognizing the reality of other people's feelings is an important part of meeting their needs and providing an environment in which they feel comfortable. I do not believe this involves adopting a management style which is masculine, or reverting to feminine wiles and manipulative strategies as an alternative. A challenge to women in management is to develop their own style, with precious few role models to whom to look, but with a confidence in all that is best in them and in their sex.

I am grateful to the Inspectorate for all that it gave me, in terms of confidence, comradeship and recognition. It gave me the confidence to move to my present job as Director of a polytechnic. I was tempted by the opportunity to get 'into the battle' rather than standing above it. I was equally tempted by the ethos of South Bank Polytechnic, with its concern for mature women and ethnic minorities, for access courses and for involvement in its inner-city community. It seemed to me to embody the values which most mattered to me, using education as a vehicle for the individual, of whatever background, to experience a sense of achievement. Most important, it was providing graduates and diplomates for the professions and for business who would be role models for others like themselves, some of whom had perhaps underachieved in school or came from backgrounds where higher education was not a traditional expectation. These considerations led me to apply for my present job, even though I knew that no woman had never been appointed to run a polytechnic, and even though I arrived for four days of interviews to discover that I was the only woman short-listed out of a group of seven candidates! It was a challenge to stay through the round of interviews, and an even greater challenge to take up the job when it was offered.

An institution of the size and complexity of South Bank Polytechnic, with a commitment to goals which ensure that life will never be easy, is an enormous challenge. Higher education itself has been through a turbulent few years in which management itself has been a new and controversial concept, and in which the twin pressures of financial accountability and expansion in student numbers and demand have imposed disciplines hitherto unknown upon those who work in universities and polytechnics. There has been little time or opportunity to reflect upon one's personal philosophy of leadership in such times, although the task would be intolerable if one had not a strong sense of personal values and style, to guide action by instinct rather than reflection in the many crises which occur. As yet I have no female counter-part for companionship: no other polytechnic or university is headed by a woman, although one hopes such a sad state of affairs will not continue for long.

I am, however, guided by a few general principles for my own way of working, although I do not reflect often on the fact that I am a woman doing a particular job at a particular time. A consciousness of being different or odd would, I believe, be a hindrance in getting on with the job, and I have always been more concerned to see things done and objectives achieved than to spend time in analysis. I also do not believe that any woman should take men as role models. It is vitally important for future generations of women that those of us who have taken on senior roles occupy them in ways that provide female role models. I am prone to say that any woman trying to be just like a man is opting to be an imitation and therefore by definition second-class. Somehow, difficult though it is, we must be ourselves. I always worry greatly when women Heads of schools or Heads of Depart-ment in higher education say to me, 'I have learned to shut the door on my family when I come to work – I'm a different person at work from what I am at home.' This seems to me to be asking of themselves more than anyone should have to ask. I have always believed that my colleagues should accept me as a totality – the mother of my children, the enthusiastic cook and hostess, as well as the HMI, polytechnic Director or whatever. In taking with me into one aspect of my life all that I am in the other, I hope thereby each is enriched.

I have said earlier that I believe the experience of parenting is one which is valuable in leadership. The experience of creating a home and a loving family team is increasingly one which is in tune with the styles of management appropriate for the 1990s. Business itself, as Walter Goldsmith and David Clutterbuck have demonstrated in their analysis of companies who survived the depression of the 1980s, has come to reject the old macho man-agement styles of the past generation. Companies which survive and thrive in the modern economy are those which achieve devolved decision-making, where people feel they have control over the day-to-day conditions of their working lives; where central management is an enabler rather than a controller; a setter of frameworks and a creator of environment and tone, rather than a conventional arbiter of staff fortunes. Goal-setting, quality control and planning are the skills of central management, while discipline and reward are rightly devolved to those closest to the everyday working lives of all in the institution.

If creativity, communication, vision, symbolism and even love are the characteristics of good management today, then this is a style of management to which women are (though of course not uniquely) well fitted. Many women (though not all) have good communication skills – a necessity in any organization where decisions have been devolved. Many women (though by no means all) have excellent antennae for the feelings and moods of those around them. This is not a comfortable talent, and many women envy men their ability to remain oblivious to the envy and resentment which any 'boss' can inspire in his or her subordinates just by being 'the boss'. Nevertheless it is a strength. The ability to see and respond to the feelings of others, and to act in accordance with those feelings, can be a valuable way to win support and motivate others.

Most of all, I believe that women can create a climate in which people feel they are trusted, in which they feel they have autonomy and control over their own lives within the constraints of outside controls with which we all live, and in which they feel they are respected as individuals. It is my own goal to create within the polytechnic the same sense of mutual trust and tolerance that is felt within the best of families, where individuals know they may make mistakes and be forgiven, because they share a common set of goals and values.

I do not apologize for 'management'. At its best, and rooted in values and goal-setting for the institution, it is the means whereby those who work in an institution are enabled to be creative, and to enjoy their work; it is thereby also the means for delivery to the student of the best service of education that our resources, well managed, enable us to give. I am concerned that many younger women now are rejecting the concept of senior management posts for themselves, either believing that there is something inherently unfeminine in a management role or rejecting the lifestyle of the woman in a senior role, which they perceive to be one of sacrifice of so many of the good and personal things in life. I cannot say too strongly that I reject the concept that management is somehow unfeminine. What is true is that the masculine style of management, which is the only model we have commonly had available for several generations, is no longer appropriate. It is for women to establish new styles of management, attractive as a role model for other women and appropriate to the needs of institutions – certainly, I would argue, most appropriate to educational institutions – in the decades that lie ahead.

Sacrifices of course there are. I have to admit defeat in discovering a way to do my job without the twelve-hour day, the six-day week and the forty-eight-week year. I am still working on ways of being more effective in fewer hours and days and weeks, and I look to the experience of other women to help me, and for us to help each other, to demonstrate that senior jobs can be done effectively and well without too high a sacrifice in one's personal and social life. I can, however, assure those women who have reservations about climbing up the management ladder that the same effort and energy can be put into preserving the quality, if not the quantity, of one's family relationships and external friendships as one puts into the job. Perhaps the best aspect of the situation lies in one's ability to help other women up the steep-sided pyramid, and I remain convinced that networks are an essential support for women as they move into posts where responsibilities and painful isolation may undermine their confidence.

Networks with other women are now much more common: the feminist revolution of the 1960s taught us to rely on each other to give the strength and confidence which women of previous generations had so sadly lacked. But the post-feminists have learned something more valuable still, and that is the lesson of partnership. In moving out into the market-place, accepting the stresses and strains that it brings, we have gained a deepened respect and affection for our menfolk who bore the heat and burden of the market-place for so many generations. We have learned how hard it is to achieve without the loving support of husbands and partners, and the loyalty and comradeship of the men with whom we work. Best of all, in moving out and away from the kitchen and nursery ourselves, we have given our menfolk the courage to move back in, within the warmth and light of the family circle.

One evening in my early, angry days, when I had coped for a whole summer with two fractious small children while my husband was working several hundred miles away, I grumbled to some neighbours that I felt a fellow-sympathy with my cat, who had just had kittens. 'Look at her,' I grumbled. 'She has no life of her own – she dares hardly rush out into the garden for two minutes before returning to the demands of her four kittens. Meanwhile, the daddy cat roams free as air outside, with not a care in the world.' My neighbour (who as it happened was a psychiatrist, although he need not have been for the purposes of this story) instantly turned my resentment on its head. 'Yes, poor daddy cat,' he said quickly. 'He is forever condemned to be shut away from the warm, loving circle that the mother cat has created with her kittens. He will never be part of the circle. Pity him, left to wander out in the cold on his own.'

His remark taught me a lesson which should not be lost. Both the world of work and the world of home are better when they are shared in equal partnership by men and women together, rather than when either tries to exclude the other. It would be a great waste of the generations of effort and hard work for women to have reached where they are today if we were to go into the next century with a failure to recognize the need for this partnership. Of course we feel some resentment at the all-male clubs, the all-male organizations, the old-boys' networks, the many, many occasions on which we find ourselves the only woman in committee, banquet, working-party or overseas mission. But the response should not be to set up all-female clubs and missions. Many women (though by no means all) have great talents in healing relationships and in creating new bridges: their involvement in public life and in the market-place should surely mean that sexism can be conquered and the human race can acknowledge the spread of its many talents through male and female alike.

I have no magic formulae to offer, other than my own conviction that women belong out in the market-place, alongside our menfolk, playing a full part in all aspects of human life. If we doubt ourselves we are lost. If we fail to remain true to our own nature and try to become imitation men, then too we are lost. Somehow, slowly and with difficulty, we must find ways to play our part which are both feminine and womanly, and which inspire respect. We do not ask for any different criteria of performance to be applied to us: we ask only to be allowed to succeed in our own way. There is nothing to be gained by dwelling on the areas of prejudice which still exist. The only way ahead is to move surefootedly, and to demonstrate by our actions that pre-judice is misplaced. The judges of our performance will be future generations, who cannot avoid marking the last half of the twentieth century as the age when women claimed – and some achieved – their human rights. Our immediate judges, of course, will be those close to us, who have shared the uncertainties as well as the triumphs, who have been big enough to allow us room to grow, and who have been willing to share with us this chapter of the human adventure.

Reference

Raskin, B. (1988) *Hot Flashes*. London, Bantam.

CHAPTER 9

A Training Initiative

ROS HARRISON and JANE WILLIAMS

Background

This chapter describes the *Women as Managers Programme* – a training-and-development initiative for women which started under the auspices of the MSC's TRIST funding in September 1986 and has since been maintained by the local education authorities in the West Midlands and by industrial sponsors. An account of the national and regional context in which the programme is set is followed by a description of its content and style and by some evaluative material from participants and from the appraisal offered after entering for the 1987 Lady Platt Award. Outcomes are explored at three levels: for the participants, for their sponsoring organization and for the LEA. The chapter ends with a summary of the key features of the programme and a look forward to future developments of the provision.

In its first year the programme catered for twelve women teachers drawn from five local authorities. The initial impetus behind the programme came from the Staff Training and Development Unit at Telford College of Arts and Technology in Shropshire. Early in the negotiation process, however, officers from the MSC and several local authority advisers contributed to the detailed planning. The programme has three aims:

- to enable a group of women teachers to enhance their professional skills,
- to increase their confidence in career planning,
- to make some impact on gender issues in the employing organization and in delivery of the curriculum.

The approach was based on a partnership arrangement between each participant, the LEA representive, the Headteacher or Principal and the programme tutor. Each named partner agreed to contribute specific elements to the programme, as an attempt to ensure integration, coherence and firm institutional and employer commitment for the individual programme and its outcomes.

The attendance pattern comprised a half-day induction, leading to an initial three-day residential, five one-day sessions over five months, and a concluding two-day residential programme. This was supplemented by individual tutorials in the participants' own work settings, for which supply cover was provided.

After a substantial initial negotiation, individual objectives for the first programme included:

- intensive self-assessment;
- a review of short-term and long-term professional-development needs, leading to an action plan;
- an exploration of current curriculum developments, particularly in relation to student-centred approaches;
- an institution-based management project.

In 1986, such a model was regarded as innovative, enterprising and uncertain, and local authority advisers were eager to consider the results of the first year's programme. The course team was encouraged by the continued involvement of several local authorities beyond the initial period of the MSC-funded project – this seemed to reflect a positive commitment to address the underrepresentation of women in senior posts.

Underrepresentation of women in educational management

Such underrepresentation of women at senior levels within schools and colleges has been well-documented. Within the West Midlands, a 1989 survey indicates the percentage of women in management posts:

Primary sector
Head 36 per cent
Deputy Head 41 per cent

Secondary sector
Head 15 per cent
Deputy Head 31 per cent
E Allowance 17 per cent
D Allowance 26 per cent

Further education sector
Principal 1 per cent
Vice-Principal 17 per cent
Head of Department 16 per cent
Principal Lecturer 18 per cent

Local education authority
Advisers 27 per cent
Advisory Teachers 30 per cent

Discussions with local-authority officers during the development of the course included consideration of a number of concerns related to this gender imbalance at senior levels. These included the need to find role models of successful women in education-based careers (given the research findings of the importance of this factor in raising pupils' aspirations); a wish to see broader short lists for senior posts, with a significant increase in female applicants; and, for some officers, a conviction that the skills and experience of many women had much to offer to the management of schools and colleges. While the programme itself did not attempt to address the structural and institutional factors in such female underrepresentation, it was designed to give a focus to maximizing the potential of targeted individual participants.

Methodology and styles

Since 1987 the programme has developed a particular character and ethos. The programme framework, operation and management components are discussed with all prospective partners at an induction meeting before the group programme begins. The commitment and support of sponsoring organizations varies, and this directly influences the effectiveness of the programme for the participants, their institution and their sponsor. Those who have benefited most have been those who were able to be fully involved through the induction meeting, the negotiation of the management project, sharing participants' experience of the group programme, and – most importantly – supporting the project through to the final presentation.

The programme content is negotiated at the initial residential weekend within the following framework:

- *Career development* – self-concept, personal assessment, role models, problem-solving;
- *Management-skills extension* – feminine and masculine management styles, assertiveness, time management and delegation, stress management.

The themes for the three one-day events are then defined. Outside contributions are invited where appropriate. The 1989/90 outline programme, for example, was as follows:

Initial residential weekend – Days 1 and 2

Aims:

- To establish the group.
- To raise awareness of relevant issues for women in education and training.
- To explore expectations of management.
- To identify links between teaching/training and management skills.
- To examine the roles women play in management.
- To provide an opportunity for individuals to develop personal goals for the course.

Day 3
Working with assertiveness (1)

Day 4
Time management and delegation
and
Tactics for promotion

Day 5
Working with assertiveness (2)
and
Stress management

Final residential weekend
The main focus of the weekend is the presentation of the management projects. Participants have the opportunity to describe briefly the issue chosen to demonstrate and develop management skills during the six-month period. A secondary focus is the significance of management style. This didactic session is used to consider the characteristics and implications of different management styles. Senior managers are invited to share in the presentations of management projects.

The process of the programme itself seeks to enhance the personal responsibility, initiative and drive of the participants. Various teaching and learning strategies are used within the group programme, such as:

- direct input;
- case studies;
- contributions from role models in education and industry;
- skills practice, with constructive feedback;
- group discussion.

Outside the group programme, the participants are encouraged to take an increased responsibility for their professional development through a number of self-development activities. These might include:

- network groups;
- discussions with senior managers and colleagues;
- mentors;
- reading;
- open learning;
- tutorials.

The programme director seeks to establish with participants an informal yet challenging learning environment. The group itself is formed at the initial residential weekend, which is held in a comfortable and peaceful hotel. Ownership of the programme results from early negotiation within a proposed framework, described earlier. Once priorities have been established, the full programme is finalized with the participants. Each one-day event begins with people sharing relevant experiences from individual work settings and individual progress with the management projects.

Part of the cohesion of the group is undoubtedly a result of the shared goal of completing a project and preparing for the final presentation. However, the relevance of shared experiences seems to be rooted in gender-related issues. These include barriers to promotion, balancing the responsibilities of work and home, and working within an organizational culture dominated by male values.

Recognition and feedback

In 1987 the programme was entered for the newly established Lady Platt Award for Equal Opportunities Training, sponsored by the Institute of Training and Development. The aim of the award scheme was to 'recognize the contribution made by organizations and individuals to equal opportunities through the design and application of good training processes'. Following a short-listing exercise, the chair of the judges' panel, Val Hammond from Ashridge Management College, visited the Unit for a detailed investigation of the programme and had an extended discussion with Jane Spratling and Ros Harrison about the aims, delivery and evaluation of the programme.

In a detailed appraisal, the judges commented on 'the sound conception and execution of the programme'. They felt that it could be offered to more women teachers and hoped that its success would encourage West Midlands authorities to expand the provision. They were also pleased to see 'early emphasis placed on monitoring the programme and carrying out some follow-up activities'. The judges' panel also noted that participants in the first programme had taken their subsequent development forward in a number of ways, including achieving promotion within their institution, moving on into the advisory service, and leading school-based in-service training on equal opportunities.

The panel encouraged the organizers to develop more substantial provision within individual local authorities. In fact, more recently course tutors and participants have supported the development of networks and programmes in several of the local authorities.

Finally, the Staff Training and Development Unit was 'highly commended' by the selection panel. Three representatives received a plaque from Lady Platt at a presentation at the Barbican in 1988.

Outcomes – personal, institutional and for sponsoring organizations

Some comments from their 'Immediate Reaction' evaluation sheets perhaps best reflect the participants' perceptions of the content and style of this programme. Given the current contact time of only seven and a half days over a six-month period, the most significant comments seem to be about the sense of a group identity. This provides a supportive network for the duration of the programme, and, for some, after the programme has formally ended. Unusually, this network includes women from the primary, secondary and FE sectors – and from industry. The linking thread is the commonality of concerns for women as managers. A psychological group is formed, as defined by Schein as any number of people who:

- interact with one another,
- are psychologically aware of one another, and
- perceive themselves to be a group.

The benefits for individuals seem to be both personal and professional:

> I most appreciated the openness of people on the course. It gave the opportunity to be objective about myself without feeling vulnerable, balanced by positive strategies and suggestions for future development.

> A most beneficial course from both a professional and a personal point of view, I learned to think positively.

On a professional level, participants cite an increased awareness and development of their skills as managers. There is recognition too of the management aspects of everyday teaching or training which have perhaps previously been undervalued. Such skills include planning, resourcing, organizing, problem-solving, evaluating, delegating, effectiveness, negotiating, coordinating and efficiency.

Formal recognition of achievement can be provided through a modular accreditation scheme offered by Crewe and Alsager College of Higher Education. The ethos of this scheme is mirrored by the *Women as Managers Programme*. The scheme handbook states that:

the central aim of the scheme is to encourage, complement and provide recognition for the professional development of those engaged in the educational system. The scheme seeks to encourage individuals to define their own needs, negotiate patterns of study, obtain recognition of prior learning and obtain credit exemption for work in other institutions. The emphasis of the scheme is on flexible and independent patterns of learning which seek to stress the partnership between the individual, employer and college.

A number of participants on the 1989/90 programme who do not have a first degree are considering modular accreditation towards a B.Ed. Retrospective Accreditation, the group programme and the management project could all be submitted for units towards this qualification.

Centrality of the management project

Given the limited contact time of the group programme, the project is the main vehicle for participants to demonstrate and develop their management skills. At the induction meeting, key questions are posed relating to:

- choosing the issue to be addressed;
- realistic time which can be set aside;
- involvement of all partners during the negotiation of the project proposal and for the duration;
- the need for a plan;
- the opportunity to tackle a non-stereotypical area of work;
- dissemination of the results;
- potential for raising one's professional and management profile.

Examples of projects within each of the education sectors and within industry are:

- *FE* – the effectiveness of the academic board;
- *Secondary* – introducing appraisal, investigation of subject choices;
- *Primary* – the Use of Ancillary Staff, designing and costing a new play area;
- *Industry* – reorganizing the Organization.

An extract from one of the evaluation questionnaires illustrates the attention given to the preparation and presentation of the project by participants:

> the final presentation of the project has to be thoroughly professional . . . every individual excelled . . . surely this is what professional development is about?

Key features

This chapter has offered a brief description of the *Women as Managers Programme* at Telford. The key features have been seen to be:

- the framework of initial *negotiation* of the programme, involving all the partners;
- the enhancement of self-confidence and self-esteem;
- mutual support in a 'safe' context, away from the workplace, where personal issues relating to conflict and stress can be resolved;
- the opportunity to undertake a 'line' project which may change the participant's 'placing' in her organization.

CHAPTER 10

Gender Issues in Management Training

HARRY GRAY

It is just over twenty years since I first became involved in offering management training to Headteachers, but it is only in the last two or three years that gender considerations have come to be taken seriously. That is not to say that previously there was never any awareness that there were both men and women Heads, but in the early years the difference was treated lightly, with a sense of friendly rivalry of the sexes. So far as I can recall, women Heads thought of themselves just as Heads, and being a Head was a fairly straightforward role, enhanced by one's being either a man or a woman. A Head was a Head, and one had simply to learn the best way of being one.

Concepts of headship

Of course, the root of the problem was that women thought of the job in a similar way to men. Essentially headship was seen as a role into which one fitted not as oneself but by becoming what was expected of you. The first dozen years of my time as a management developer were largely concerned with trying to help Heads to understand that they had to fill the position of Head in their own special way – that one could not become the ideal person at the moment of appointment but that one had to discover how one could best do the job through one's own strengths and personality. For many Heads in the 1970s the key problem was a denial of themselves in order to fill a role impersonally. There was much talk of objectivity in the performance of the job, as if one became another kind of being in the role. I believe both men and women felt the pressure to become an ideal type of Head to such an extent that the acceptibility of differences was a forbidden topic.

Yet, of course, there were differences between individual men and women, and there were some generalized differences between men and women as a whole. As our understanding of gender issues has developed, we have moved from considering men and women as two great, opposed sexual blocks to realizing that differences within each sex are much greater than those between the sexes and that a simple view that all men or all women fall into one category of behaviour is quite false. Whatever the history of gender relationships, there is something much more complex in relationships that involve individuals and their self-concept as well as their identification with gender, and the implications of this will be discussed later. However, in the early days of my work with Heads the main awareness on the part of women was that they were in competition with men both for the jobs themselves (this being a period of growing mixed and comprehensive schooling) and in the evaluation of performance.

Characteristics of the school system

It needs to be remembered that the English and Welsh school system – it may also be true of the Scottish system, but I have little experience of that – is one of remarkable uniformity, perhaps because of the fact that it has always been a central system locally delivered. Secondary education has been structured around the highly competitive university-entrance requirements that have been transmuted into what is now the GCSE. Successful schools are schools which are successful in competition with other schools, and the simple measure of success is examination results. Comprehensive schooling has not managed to change the popular criteria of success, even though many of the schools themselves have concentrated on other aspects of education. It has generally been considered that competitiveness (or, at least, certain forms of it) is a masculine quality, and therefore running a school is likely to demand qualities possessed by men rather than by women.

Though this is a naïve view of gender, it is nevertheless the way in which many Heads think of the running of their school, and women Heads get caught up in the same perceptions. Women Heads felt that they had to show themselves as good as the men on the same measures, and this meant that much of their personal effort went into showing that they were as good at headship as the men – indeed, that they were better than the men on male criteria but with an added quality of traditional femininity (that is, there were more vases of flowers in the school). But male Heads too were caught up in this general macho view of headship, and we were just coming to the end of a period when education was characterized by a number of publicity-conscious Heads who stumped around the country telling everyone just how running a school should be done. These were 'heady' days for change and reform, but the energy put into change was exceedingly macho and there was little time for patient and considered development.

Management as certainty

The Heads who came on my course wanted to know the answers that management and industry could give (though they left me in no doubt that schools were different – a somewhat paradoxical stance). They were nonplussed when they found that I had no answers but asked them to join in a process of experiment and reflection about what they were doing as managers. This is what industrialists would understand as management development, but Heads found it a particularly threatening approach. Because of the lack of preparation and training for headship, by the time seasoned Heads came on management courses they brought with them a considerable period of personal practice that was up for analysis and criticism. No wonder they felt vulnerable. Much of their behaviour was defensive – sometimes aggressive – and they found it easier to talk about what other Heads or teachers needed rather than what they themselves could identify as personal needs.

This refusal to open up about themselves was highlighted very clearly with a group of a dozen Heads I was working with in a series of eight weekly sessions. All of the Heads were from the same LEA, and they were therefore highly defensive about themselves. We were trying to get into the relationship between the Heads and their Deputies (which I still find to be the most distressing area of relationships in secondary-school management).

They all complained about their Deputies at great length, except for the few cases where the Deputy could do absolutely no wrong – clear black-and-white judgements. But there was one woman Head on the course who tried to open up about her relationships, only to be cut off by the men, who could not bear to have personal relationships brought out into the open.

Gender and emotional awareness

My tendency would have been to note this as a difference between men and women, but I now know that differences are not so clearly differentiated. What is clear, however, is that it was thought unprofessional to deal with emotional issues: the preference was to try to remain 'objective'. Of course this is non-sense. The plea for objectivity is often a way of blocking the confrontation of the affective realities of organizations and preventing a personal reflective process. Women may be as ready to block as men, and the ethos of school management has been one that encourages Heads to perceive themselves as the most objective and least emotional members of staff. In later years I have come to find some women quite unable to talk about themselves in their relationships with their colleagues, and some men very able to do so. Having said this, schools are still places where gender issues are a sensitive area.

The school as a family

I have recently undertaken some long-term interventions in schools in which I worked as a management consultant for about a year. My main concern was to help to build a creative dialogue among and within the various management levels of each school. I discovered that one way of understanding the basic organizational dynamics of the school was to recognize that people behave according to a familiar model; that is, the school is organized as a large family of which the Head is either mother or father. Other members of the school cannot be other than children or relatives, and of course they cannot change their basic relationship. In most cases this means that no one is allowed to grow up. Deputies are simply older children who are not yet

ready to leave home, and everyone behaves in a family relationship to everyone else. Much of the frustration that Deputies feel is
a consequence of their not being allowed to be adults in the eyes
of the Head. I do not want to press this analogy here, because a
full working-out is not appropriate, but the important insight
from the model is that it explains just how schools are gender-
based in their organization.

What appears to happen is that the Head behaves according to
his or her own self-concept in both sex and gender terms. Consequently, other members of the organization have to respond to
the Head in similar, complementary, terms. The impact of the
Head's behaviour is greatest on his or her adult staff, but in some
schools (especially primary schools) the children are directly
affected too. Heads behave both in terms of their sense of gender
(that is, of appropriate gender behaviour as well as personal
gender identity) and also in terms of their sexual identity. In both
cases there will be both acceptance and denial. For example, a
woman Head may deny her feminine qualities and always try to
be tough, although her natural inclinations are to be nurturing.
Or she may deny that she finds a male member of staff sexually
attractive, although she frequently rewards him for good behaviour. The same happens with male Heads who deny that they are
biased against women even though the organizational structure
indicates that they are.

Pastoral role of women

The position of women in senior management positions in school
is significant. In primary schools, the majority of Heads are men
and the role of Deputy is uncertain and often ambiguous. In
secondary schools, women are in a minority so far as Head and
Deputy positions are concerned. Women Deputies tend to fill
pastoral roles, and I know of only a few schools where the key
pastoral role is filled by a man. Often women are reluctant to see
themselves as Deputies but have preferred to be 'Senior Mistress',
which implies limited responsibilities in senior management. My
guess is that this is most often the case where the woman has been
promoted within the school rather than when she has applied for
the post as part of a conscious career plan. Occupancy of the
position of Head of Department is still severely gender-biased,

though this may have more to do with the career structure of the profession than with organizational values.

I find the familial model with its sex and gender dimensions very helpful in understanding organizational behaviour in schools and colleges because it gets away from the kind of gender stereotyping which has become so sterile when it comes to the practicalities of trying to change gender biases, as in the case of equal opportunities. It is, however, useful for diagnostic purposes to use a pair of gender paradigms which represent the traditional dichotomy of gender characteristics. I have used them quite successfully with teachers to open up discussion about gender issues, and have then been able to move to an exploration of personal attitudes to gender. I have used the conventional masculine and feminine paradigms to illustrate conventional prejudices, though I have changed the titles to 'defensive/aggressive' and 'nurturing'.

Gender paradigms

The nurturing paradigm broadly defines the feminine aspects of personality in terms such as:

- caring,
- creative,
- intuitive,
- aware of individual differences,
- non-competitive,
- tolerant,
- subjective,
- informal.

The defensive/aggressive paradigm broadly defines aspects of personality in terms such as

- highly regulated,
- conformist,
- normative,
- competitive,
- evaluative,
- disciplined,
- objective,
- formal.

I use the term 'defensive/aggressive' to indicate that the second paradigm helps the individual to protect himself from being emotionally exposed and is outwardly directed rather than inwardly reflective. It is a defence against self-awareness, and its aggressive forms are intended to pre-empt personal disclosure.

Teacher reactions to gender issues

If I use these paradigms with large mixed groups of teachers, I invariably get very positive reactions from women, leading to excited discussion, but from men I receive not so much a negative response as an indifferent one. It therefore seems to me that women are much more aware of gender issues at a quite complex level, but that men are nonplussed when these issues are raised. It also seems to be true that, even when men are interested in gender issues, they misunderstand the issues and simply see women as a repressed minority who ought not to be repressed, but without understanding the psychological issue of gender and sexuality. Indeed, many women nowadays are changing their views about gender issues and are coming to see them not so much as political but as personal – as requiring organizational solutions, but not simply as issues of administrative equality.

I use these paradigms as a teaching aid. They provide an entry to the use of other paradigms that are generally volunteered by the group members, who may for instance recall the Jungian concepts of animus and anima, of *logos* and *eros*. I have never intended them to be exact paradigms for gender difference because I do not believe that there are clear attitudinal differences between the genders, though there may be historically engendered characteristic attitudes.

Reasons for the history of gender attitudes

I do not want to deny the history of gender inequality in education or anywhere else, but it is important to recognize that the reasons for our history need to be explained, and a helpful form of explanation comes from an understanding of how individuals come to have a sense of gender identity. Critical to a sense of gender identity is a sense of sexual identity – and this is the crucial issue with Heads of schools. My definition of gender is that it is a description of social roles, whereas sexual identity is a definition of how one feels about oneself. One's sex is given, but one's gender is a choice. Many male Heads feel the need to deny their sexual self, and they do this by falling into the gender stereotype which they believe gives them objectivity. By 'sexual self' I mean the sense of self that recognizes that one is a man or a woman and then accepts the ways in which one is a man or a woman in one's social relationships. For example, some people find it hard to express feelings of tenderness in a physical way; this is not a matter of gender, because both men and women have this difficulty, but it is a matter of gender as to how it is expressed. Conventionally, women may touch one another while men may not, except in sporting environments.

Women's awareness is greater than men's

In my more recent work with Heads, matters of gender and sexuality have become increasingly important. Issues are raised and dealt with with some thoroughness. In a recent course, issues of gender were raised by the women members, and the men were forced to respond. The interesting aspect of their response was that it was soon concerned less with 'equality' issues than with questions of sexuality. The men were faced with the fact that the women were more free to express themselves as people than the men were, and that was because the men felt that some behaviours were not proper to their manliness even though they felt drawn in certain directions. Entry to the questions of sexuality came through the variety of dress the women chose over a period of several weeks. The men tended to dress in a similar way all the time, but the women came in a considerable variation of clothes according to how they felt that day or what their activities were. This raised questions of how one felt about oneself in social situations. In gender terms, the men admitted that they often felt that the nurturing paradigm was more true of them than the macho (defensive/ aggressive) one, and this raised issues of their sexuality.

Men's failure to understand themselves

It seems clear that for many men the reasons for the way they treat women as different arise less from a sense of superiority than from a lack of understanding of themselves. Men feel constrained to behave like men, and that means treating women as women. Since men do not allow other men to deviate very far from a male norm, men find it hard to accept themselves – the condition on which acceptance of others is possible. As a matter of fact, women have open to them more gender-acceptable lifestyles than do men. Merely in the matter of clothes, women may dress in a greater variety of styles than men. Indeed 'cross-dressing' for women is merely a matter of style, while for men it is a sexual transgression – as we know from the problem of transvestism, which does not exist for women, since they may dress as they like without social stigma. We can see this in schools where girls can wear boy's clothes (some private schools have items in their uniform which are very 'butch') but boys cannot wear girls' – for example in sportswear.

Gender-consciousness in schools

Schools are very gender-conscious. The move to equality of opportunity with regard to the curriculum is hesitant: there are still 'boys' subjects' and 'girls' subjects'. Underlying this is the fear of sexuality. Gender restraints on both boys and girls are rigorous, and teachers find it difficult to cope with feminine boys and masculine girls. The insistence on school uniform would seem to arise out of fear of individuality, and enforced wearing of uniform suppresses sexual expression. Of course, children manage to personalize their uniform, and some of the personalizing is overtly sexual. Girls' uniform is often very unfeminine, and boys' uniform often expresses a military repression. The greater the insistence on uniform, the greater the suspicion of sexual repression on the part of the enforcers.

It is my view that there is an underlying fear of sexuality in both the family and the school. Because schools model themselves on the family (*in loco parentis*), they are vulnerable to the sexual problems and fears of families. Where adults and children are together there are incredible social anxieties. To keep men and women, boys and girls, severely separated in gender terms is one way of avoiding sexual issues, yet paradoxically it may serve only to exacerbate them. Schools are very much predicated on the need to control children, and, as in all situations where control is almost the *raison d'être* – like prisons – the very matters that are most feared become activated. Schools use crude gender paradigms to control their members, and so their probems arise in gender forms – such as the unequal treatment of boys and girls, men and women, and the concentration on certain forms of achievement rather than others.

Organizational forms and gender paradigms

Schools could be quite different from what they are if they would change their organizational paradigms. If they were more caring and nurturing of individuals, more concerned with individual growth and development, more able to recognize the creative worth of differences rather than requiring uniformity or at best controlled variety (such as having boys playing the parts of girls in school plays in all-boys schools!), more able to recognize people as people without preconceptions about what is right and proper, they would be not only different places but more effective in their social and academic role. Reinforcing gender prejudices is a way of avoiding the realities of human life and the role that schools can play in the development and maturation of society. It is sad that schools are so concerned with quantitative achievement rather than the quality of personal life. Gender confusion in education is a major measure of how schools fail. Gender stereotyping is the means of avoiding the realities of sexuality and the importance of individuality.

As Heads become more aware of the importance of gender issues in schools, there will be a change in the way men and women think about one another and how teachers think about children. If we are to learn to live and work together in an open and creative way, we must learn to respect individual differences that concern our sexual and gender orientations as much as our intellectual abilities. The ultimate question is not one of the nature of two monolithic sexes or genders but how well we understand the ways in which people can learn to be self-accepting people who also tolerate the self-acceptance of others.

Index